A Critical Assessment of Romantic Literature

A Critical Assessment of Romantic Literature

C. Jagannath

SWASTIK

SWASTIK PUBLICATIONS
DELHI - 110 094 (INDIA)

A CRITICAL ASSESSMENT OF ROMANTIC LITERATURE

First Published 2011

ISBN 978-93-80138-91-6

Published in India by

SWASTIK PUBLICATIONS
31, Gali No. 1, A-Block, Pocket-5,
CRP Water Tank, Sonia Vihar
Delhi-110094 (INDIA)
email: swastik_books@yahoo.com

Printed at: Deepak Offset Press, Delhi.

Contents

Preface

"Tell me not in mournful numbers,
Life is but an empty dream
Life is real! Life is earnest!
And the grave is not its goal."

—*Longfellow*

Major political and social changes at the end of the 18th century, particularly the French Revolution, prompted a new breed of writing known as Romanticism. William Wordsworth and Samuel Taylor Coleridge began the trend for bringing emotionalism and introspection to English literature, with a new concentration on the individual and the common man. The reaction to urbanism and industrialisation prompted poets to explore nature, for example the Lake Poets.

The main poets of this movement were William Blake, William Wordsworth, Samuel Taylor Coleridge, Percy Bysshe Shelley, Lord Byron, and John Keats. The birth of English Romanticism is often dated to the publication in 1798 of Wordsworth and Coleridge's *Lyrical Ballads*. However, Blake had been publishing since the early 1780s. Much of the focus on Blake only came about during the last century when Northrop Frye discussed his work in his book "The Anatomy of Criticism." Shelley is most famous for such classic anthology verse works as *Ozymandias*, and long visionary poems which include *Prometheus Unbound*. Shelley's groundbreaking poem *The Masque of Anarchy* calls for nonviolence in protest and political action. It is perhaps the first modern statement of the principle of nonviolent protest .

Additionally, the Romantic movement marked a shift in the use of language. Attempting to express the "language of the common man", Wordsworth and his fellow Romantic poets focused on employing poetic language for a wider audience, countering the mimetic, tightly constrained Neo-Classic poems (although it's important to note that the poet wrote first and foremost for his/her own creative, expression). In Shelley's "Defense of Poetry", he contends that poets are the "creators of language" and that the poet's job is to refresh language for their society. The Romantics were not the only poets of note at this time. In the work of John Clare the late Augustan voice is blended with a peasant's first-hand knowledge to produce arguably some of the finest nature poetry in the English language. Another contemporary poet who does not fit into the Romantic group was Walter Savage Landor. Landor was a classicist whose poetry forms a link between the Augustans and Robert Browning, who much admired it.

This book is devised as a compact handbook of reference for students, researchers and teachers of English literature besides general readers. The vital information is contained under the following chapters—Introduction; English Romanticism: An Overview; The Augustans; Romanticism Amidst Spenserians; Thomas Warton and His School; The Landscape Poets; Representative Writers; Conclusion; Appendix; Glossary and Bibliography etc.

Hopefully, this will serve the purpose of all those for whom this is meant.

We have consulted a number of authoritative works in course of working on this. We owe a deep sense of gratitude to all those scholars whose views and works make core of the present endeavour. I am equally grateful to my friends and family members for their enthusiastic cooperation and inspiration. My publishers deserve all appreciation for materialising the present venture superbly, that two within shortest possible time.

Suggestions, constructive criticism and comments are welcome from all learned scholars to enhance the quality of information contained in this work, which will be corroborated in subsequent edition with due acknowledgement.

—C.J.

1
Introduction

Before proceeding to romanticism and romantic literature, first let us have a look at contemporary history and its influence on literature.

Major political and social changes at the end of the 18th century, particularly the French Revolution, prompted a new breed of writing known as Romanticism. William Wordsworth and Samuel Taylor Coleridge began the trend for bringing emotionalism and introspection to English literature, with a new concentration on the individual and the common man. The reaction to urbanism and industrialisation prompted poets to explore nature, for example the Lake Poets.

The third major Lake poet, Robert Southey, enjoys lasting popularity, although perhaps his most enduring contribution to literary history is the immortal children's classic, *The Story of the Three Bears*, the basis of the original *Goldilocks* story. Around the same period, the iconoclastic printer William Blake, largely disconnected from the major streams of elite literature of the time, was constructing his own highly idiosyncratic poetic creations, while the Scottish nationalist poet Robert Burns was collecting and adapting the folk songs of Scotland into a body of national poetry for his homeland.

The major "second generation" Romantic poets included George Gordon Byron (Lord Byron). They flouted social convention and often used poetry as a political voice. Amongst Lord Byron's best-known works are the brief poems *She Walks in Beauty*, *When We Two Parted*, and *So, we'll go no more a roving*, in addition to narrative poems *Childe Harold's Pilgrimage* and *Don Juan*. Another key poet of the Romantic movement was John Keats, whose poems such as *Ode to a Nightingale* expound on his aesthetic theory of negative capability, and remain among the most celebrated by any author of the period. *To Autumn* is the final work in a collection of poems known as "Keats's 1819 odes". Percy Shelley, famous for his association with Keats and Byron, was the third major romantic poet of the second generation. Critically regarded as among the finest lyric poets in the English language, Shelley is most famous for such widely anthologized verse works as *Ozymandias*, and long visionary poems which include *Prometheus Unbound*. Shelley's groundbreaking poem *The Masque of Anarchy* calls for nonviolence in protest and political action. It is perhaps the first modern statement of the principle of nonviolent protest. Mahatma Gandhi's passive resistance was influenced and inspired by Shelley's verse, and Gandhi would often quote the poem to vast audiences.

The Romantic Movement

The last quarter of the 18th century was a time of social and political turbulence, with revolutions in the United States, France, Ireland and elsewhere. In Great Britain, movement for social change and a more inclusive sharing of power was also growing. This was the backdrop against which the Romantic movement in English poetry emerged.

The main poets of this movement were William Blake, William Wordsworth, Samuel Taylor Coleridge, Percy Bysshe Shelley, Lord Byron, and John Keats. The birth of English Romanticism is often dated to the publication in 1798 of Wordsworth and Coleridge's *Lyrical Ballads*. However, Blake had been publishing since the early 1780s. Much of the focus on Blake only came about during the last century when Northrop Frye discussed his work in his book "The Anatomy of Criticism." Shelley is most famous for such classic anthology verse works as *Ozymandias*, and long visionary poems which include *Prometheus Unbound*. Shelley's groundbreaking poem *The Masque of Anarchy* calls for nonviolence in protest and political action. It is perhaps the first modern statement of the principle of nonviolent protest. Mahatma Gandhi's passive resistance was influenced and inspired by Shelley's verse, and would often quote the poem to vast audiences.

In poetry, the Romantic movement emphasised the creative expression of the individual and the need to find and formulate new forms of expression. The Romantics, with the partial exception of Byron, rejected the poetic ideals of the eighteenth century, and each of them returned to Milton for inspiration, though each drew something different from Milton. They also put a good deal of stress on their own originality. To the Romantics, the moment of creation was the most important in poetic expression and could not be repeated once it passed. Because of this new emphasis, poems that were not complete were nonetheless included in a poet's body of work (such as Coleridge's "Kubla Khan" and "Christabel").

Additionally, the Romantic movement marked a shift in the use of language. Attempting to express the "language of the common man", Wordsworth and his fellow Romantic poets focused on employing poetic language for a wider audience, countering the mimetic, tightly constrained Neo-Classic poems (although it's important to note that the poet wrote first and foremost for his/her own creative, expression). In Shelley's "Defense of Poetry", he contends that poets are the "creators of language" and that the poet's job is to refresh language for their society. The Romantics were not the only poets of note at this time. In the work of John Clare the late Augustan voice is blended with a peasant's first-hand knowledge to produce arguably some of the finest nature poetry in the English language. Another contemporary poet who does not fit into the Romantic group was Walter Savage Landor. Landor was a classicist whose poetry forms a link between the Augustans and Robert Browning, who much admired it.

The Victorian era was a period of great political change, social and economic change. The Empire recovered from the loss of the American colonies and entered a period of rapid expansion. This expansion, combined with increasing industrialisation and mechanisation, led to a prolonged period of economic growth. The Reform Act 1832 was the beginning of a process that would eventually lead to universal suffrage.

The major High Victorian poets were Alfred, Lord Tennyson, Robert Browning, Elizabeth Barrett Browning, Matthew Arnold and Gerard Manley Hopkins. Tennyson was, to some degree, the Spenser of the new age and his *Idylls of the Kings* can be read as a Victorian version of *The Faerie Queen*, that is as a poem that sets out to provide a mythic foundation to the idea of empire.

The Brownings spent much of their time out of England and explored European models and matter in much of their poetry. Robert Browning's great innovation was the dramatic monologue, which he used to its full extent in his long novel in verse, *The Ring and the Book*. Elizabeth Barrett Browning is perhaps best remembered for *Sonnets from the Portuguese* but her long poem *Aurora Leigh* is one of the classics of 19th century feminist literature. Matthew Arnold was much influenced by Wordsworth, though his poem *Dover Beach* is often considered a precursor of the modernist revolution. Hopkins wrote in relative obscurity and his work was not published until after his death. His unusual style (involving what he called "sprung rhythm" and heavy reliance on rhyme and alliteration) had a considerable influence on many of the poets of the 1940s.

The Pre-Raphaelite Brotherhood was a mid-19th century arts movement dedicated to the reform of what they considered the sloppy Mannerist painting of the day. Although primarily concerned with the visual arts, two members, the brother and sister Dante Gabriel Rossetti and Christina Rossetti, were also poets of some ability. Their poetry shares many of the concerns of the painters; an interest in Medieval models, an almost obsessive attention to visual detail and an occasional tendency to lapse into whimsy. Dante Rossetti worked with, and had some influence on, the leading Arts and crafts painter and poet William Morris. Morris shared the Pre-Raphaelite interest in the poetry of the European Middle Ages, to the point of producing some illuminated manuscript volumes of his work.

Towards the end of the century, English poets began to take an interest in French symbolism and Victorian poetry entered a decadent *fin-de-siecle* phase. Two groups of poets emerged, the *Yellow Book* poets who adhered to the tenets of Aestheticism, including Algernon Charles Swinburne, Oscar Wilde and Arthur Symons and the Rhymer's Club group that included Ernest Dowson, Lionel Johnson and William Butler Yeats.

Comic Verse

Comic verse abounded in the Victorian era. Magazines such as *Punch magazine* and *Fun magazine* teemed with humorous invention and were aimed at a well-educated readership. The most famous collection of Victorian comic verse is the Bab Ballads.

The 19th Century Novel

At the same time, Jane Austen was writing highly polished novels about the life of the landed gentry, seen from a woman's point of view, and wryly focused on practical social issues, especially marriage and money. Austen's *Pride and Prejudice* 1813, is often considered the epitome of the romance genre, and some of her other most notable works include; *Sense and Sensibility*, *Mansfield Park*, *Persuasion* and *Emma*

Walter Scott's novel-writing career was launched in 1814 with *Waverley*, often called the first historical novel, and was followed by *Ivanhoe*. His popularity in England and further abroad did much to form the modern stereotype of Scottish culture. Other novels by Scott which contributed to the image of him as a Scottish patriot include *Rob Roy*. Scott was the highest earning and most popular author up to that time.

Mary Shelley is best known for her novel *Frankenstein* 1818, infusing elements of the Gothic novel and Romantic movement. Frankenstein's chilling tale suggests modern organ transplants, tissue regeneration, that remind readers of the moral issues raised by today's medicine.

John William Polidori wrote *The Vampyre* 1819, creating the literary vampire genre. His short story was inspired by the life of Lord Byron and his poem *The Giaour*. Another major influence on vampire fiction is *Varney the Vampire* 1845, where many standard Vampire features originated — Varney has fangs, leaves two puncture wounds on the neck of his victims, has hypnotic powers, superhuman strength, and was also the first example of the "sympathetic vampire", who loathes his condition but is a slave to it.

From the mid-1820s until the 1840s, fashionable novels depicting the lives of the upper class in an indiscreet manner, identifying the real people whom the characters were based, dominated the market. It was in the Victorian era (1837–1901) that the novel became the leading form of literature in English. Most writers were now more concerned to meet the tastes of a large middle-class reading public than to please aristocratic patrons. The 1830s saw a resurgence of the social novel, where sensationalized accounts and stories of the working class poor were directed toward middle class audiences to incite sympathy and action towards pushing for legal and moral change. Elizabeth Gaskell's *North and*

South contrasts the lifestyle in the industrial north of England with the wealthier south.

Sir John Barrow's descriptive 1831 account of the Mutiny on the Bounty immortalised the Royal Navy ship HMS Bounty and her people. The legend of Dick Turpin was popularized when the 18th century English highwayman's exploits appeared in the novel *Rookwood* in 1834.

Charles Dickens emerged on the literary scene in the 1830s, confirming the trend for serial publication. Dickens wrote vividly about London life and struggles of the poor, often, as in *Oliver Twist*, employing a popular style which would prove accessible to readers of all classes. The festive tale *A Christmas Carol* he called his "little Christmas book". *Great Expectations* is a quest for maturity. *A Tale of Two Cities* is set in London and Paris. Dickens early works are masterpieces of comedy, such as *The Pickwick Papers*. Later his works became darker, without losing his genius for caricature.

The emotionally powerful works of the Brontë sisters: Charlotte's *Jane Eyre*, Emily's *Wuthering Heights* and Anne's *Agnes Grey* were released in 1847 after their search to secure publishers. William Makepeace Thackeray's satirised British society in *Vanity Fair* 1847, while Anthony Trollope's novels portrayed the lives of the landowning and professional classes of early Victorian England.

Although pre-dated by John Ruskin's *The King of the Golden River* in 1841, the history of the modern fantasy genre is generally said to begin with George MacDonald, influential author of *The Princess and the Goblin* and *Phantastes* 1858. William Morris was a popular English poet who wrote several fantasy novels during the latter part of the 19th century.

Literature for children was published during the Victorian period, some of which has become globally well-known, such as the works of Lewis Carroll, notably *Alice's*

Adventures in Wonderland, while Anna Sewell wrote the classic animal novel *Black Beauty*.

Wilkie Collins epistolary novel *The Moonstone* 1868, is generally considered the first detective novel in the English language. *The Woman in White* is regarded as one of the finest sensation novels. The novels of George Eliot, such as *Middlemarch*, were a milestone of literary realism, and combine high Victorian literary detail with an intellectual breadth that removes them from the narrow confines they often depict. Novels of Thomas Hardy and others, dealt with the changing social and economic situation of the countryside. Penny dreadful publications were an alternative to mainstream works, and were aimed at working class adolescents, introducing the infamous Sweeney Todd. The premier ghost story writer of the 19th century was Sheridan Le Fanu.

His works include the macabre mystery novel *Uncle Silas* 1865, and his Gothic novella *Carmilla* 1872, tells the story of a young woman's susceptibility to the attentions of a female vampire. Bram Stoker, author of seminal horror work *Dracula*, featured as its primary antagonist the vampire Count Dracula, with the vampire hunter Abraham Van Helsing his arch-enemy. *Dracula* has been attributed to a number of literary genres including vampire literature, horror fiction, gothic novel and invasion literature.

H. G. Wells, who alongside Jules Verne, is referred to as "The Father of Science Fiction", invented a number of themes that are now classic in the science fiction genre. *The War of the Worlds* 1898, describing an invasion of late Victorian England by Martians using tripod fighting machines equipped with advanced weaponry, is a seminal depiction of an alien invasion of Earth. *The Time Machine* is generally credited with the popularization of the concept of time travel using a vehicle that allows an operator to travel purposefully and selectively. The term "*time machine*" coined by Wells, is now universally used to refer to such a vehicle. Sir Arthur Conan Doyle's Sherlock Holmes is a brilliant London-based "consulting detective", famous for his intellectual prowess, skillful use of astute observation, deductive reasoning and forensic skills to solve difficult cases. Holmes' archenemy Professor Moriarty, is widely considered to be the first true example of a supervillain, while Sherlock Holmes has become a by-word for a detective. Conan Doyle wrote four novels and fifty-six short stories featuring Holmes, from 1880 up to 1907, with a final case in 1914. All but four Conan Doyle stories are narrated by Holmes' friend, assistant, and biographer, Dr. John H. Watson.

The Lost World literary genre was inspired by real stories of archaeological discoveries by imperial adventurers. H. Rider Haggard wrote one of the earliest examples, *King Solomon's Mines* in 1885. Contemporary European politics and diplomatic manoeuvrings informed Anthony Hope's swashbuckling Ruritanian adventure novels *The Prisoner of Zenda* 1894, and *Rupert of Hentzau*, 1898. A. F. Anstey's comic novel *Vice Versa* 1882, sees a father and son magically switch bodies. Satirist Jerome K. Jerome's *Three Men in a Boat* 1889, is a humorous account of a boating holiday on the river Thames. Grossmith brothers George & Weedon's *Diary of a Nobody* 1892, is also considered a classic work of humour.

In the latter years of the 19th century, precursors of the modern picture book were illustrated books of poems and short stories produced by English illustrators Randolph Caldecott, Walter Crane, and Kate Greenaway. These had a larger proportion of pictures to words than earlier books, and many of their pictures were in colour. Some British artists made their living illustrating novels and children's books, include Arthur Rackham, Cicely Mary Barker, W. Heath Robinson, Henry J. Ford, John Leech, and George Cruikshank. One of the earliest and most influential books with the format that modern picture books retain is Beatrix Potter's *The Tale of Peter Rabbit*.

An important forerunner of modernist literature, Joseph Conrad wrote the novel *Heart of Darkness* 1899, a symbolic story within a story or frame narrative about an Englishman Marlow's foreign assignment, that is widely regarded as a significant work of English literature and part of the Western canon.

2

English Romanticism: An Overview

To begin with, Romanticism is a comprehensive term for all the various tendencies towards change observable in European literature, art and culture in the later 18th century and early 19th century. In fact Romanticism was not a unified movement with a clearly agreed agenda, and its emphases varied widely according to time, place and individual author.

What is, or was, romanticism? or, at least, What is, or was English romanticism? There are words which connote so much, which take up into themselves so much of the history of the human mind, that any compendious explanation of their meaning—any definition which is not, at the same time, a rather extended description—must serve little other end than to supply a convenient mark of identification. How can we define in a sentence words like renaissance, philistine, sentimentalism, transcendental, Bohemia, pre-Raphaelite, impressionist, realistic? It may be possible to hit upon a form of words which will mark romanticism off from everything else—tell in a clause what it is *not*; but to add a positive content to the definition—to tell what romanticism *is*, will require a very different and more gradual process. Nevertheless a rough, working definition may be useful to start with. Romanticism, then, in the sense in means the reproduction in modern art or literature of the life and thought of the Middle Ages.

Some other elements will have to be added to this

definition, and some modifications of it will suggest themselves from time to time. It is provisional, tentative, classic, but will serve our turn till we are ready to substitute a better. It is the definition which Heine gives in his brilliant little book on the Romantic School in Germany.

"All the poetry of the Middle Ages," he adds, "has a certain definite character, through which it differs from the poetry of the Greeks and Romans. In reference to this difference, the former is called Romantic, the latter Classic. These names, however, are misleading, and have hitherto caused the most vexatious confusion."

Meanwhile the passage recalls the fact that *romantic*, when used as a term in literary nomenclature, is not an independent, but a referential word. It implies its opposite, the classic; and the ingenuity of critics has been taxed to its uttermost to explain and develop the numerous points of contrast. To form a thorough conception of the romantic, therefore, we must also form some conception of the classic.

Now there is an obvious unlikeness between the thought and art of the nations of pagan antiquity and the thought and art of the peoples of Christian, feudal Europe. Everyone will agree to call the Parthenon, the "Diana" of the Louvre, the "Oedipus" of Sophocles, the orations of Demosthenes classical; and to call the cathedral of Chartres, the walls of Nuremberg—*die Perle des Mittelalters*—the "Legenda Aurea" of Jacobus de Voragine, the "Tristan und Isolde" of Gottfried of Strasburg, and the illuminations in a Catholic missal of the thirteenth century romantic. The same unlikeness is found between modern works conceived in the spirit, or executed in direct imitation, of ancient and medieval art respectively.

It is easy to decide that Flaxman's outline drawings in illustration of Homer are classic; that Alfieri's tragedies, Goethe's "Iphigenie auf Tauris" Landor's "Hellenics," Gibson's statues, David's paintings, and the church of the Madeleine in Paris are classical, at least in intentions and in the models which they follow; while Victor Hugo's "Notre Dame de Paris," Scott's "Ivanhoe," Fouqué's "Der Zauberring," and Rossetti's painting, "The Girlhood of Mary," are no less certainly romantic in their inspiration. But critics have given a wider extension than this to the terms classic and romantic. They have discerned, or imagined, certain qualities, attitudes of mind, ways of thinking and feeling, traits of style which distinguish classic from romantic art; and they have applied the words accordingly to work which is not necessarily either antique or medieval in subject.

Thus it is assumed, for example, that the productions of Greek and Roman genius were characterized by clearness, simplicity, restraint, unity of design, subordination of the part to the whole; and therefore modern works which make this impression of noble plainness and severity, of harmony in construction, economy of means and clear, definite outline, are often spoken of as classical, quite irrespective of the historical period which they have to do with. In this sense, it is usual to say that Wordsworth's "Michael" is classical, or that Goethe's "Hermann and Dorothea" is classical; though Wordsworth may be celebrating the virtues of a Westmoreland shepherd, and Goethe telling the story of two rustic lovers on the German border at the time of the Napoleonic wars. On the other hand, it is asserted that the work of mediaeval poets and artists is marked by an excess of sentiment, by over-lavish decoration, a strong sense of color and a feeble sense of form, an attention to detail, at the cost of the main impression, and a consequent tendency to run into the exaggerated, the fantastic, and the grotesque.

It is not uncommon, therefore, to find poets like Byron and Shelly classified as romanticists, by virtue of their possession of these, or similar, characteristics, although no one could be more remote from medieval habits of thought than the author of "Don Juan" or the author of "The Revolt of Islam." But the extension of these opposing terms to the work of writers who have so little in common with either the antique or the medieval as Wordsworth, on the one hand, and Byron, on the other, does not stop here. It is one of the embarrassments of the literary historian that nearly every word which he uses has two meanings, a critical and a popular meaning. In common speech, classic has come to signify almost anything that is good.

If we look in our dictionaries we find it defined somewhat in this way: "Conforming to the best authority in literature and art; pure; chaste; refined; originally and chiefly used of the best Greek and Roman writers, but also applied to the best modern authors, or their works." "Classic, *n.* A work of acknowledged excellence and authority." In this sense of the word, "Robinson Crusoe" is a classic; the "Pilgrim's Progress" is a classic; every piece of literature which is customarily recommended as a safe pattern for young writers to form their style upon is a classic. Contrariwise the word *romantic*, as popularly employed, expresses a shade of disapprobation. The dictionaries make it a synonym for *sentimental, fanciful, wild, extravagant, chimerical*, all evident derivatives from their more critical definition, "pertaining or appropriate to the style of the Christian and popular literature of the Middle Ages, as opposed to the classical antique." The etymology of *romance* is familiar. The various dialects which sprang from the corruption of the Latin were called by the common name of *romans*. The name was then applied to any piece of literature composed in this vernacular instead of in the ancient classical Latin. And as the favorite kind of writing in Provençal, Old French, and Spanish was the tale of chivalrous adventure that was called *par excellence, a roman, romans*, or romance.

The adjective *romantic* is much later, implying, as it does, a certain degree of critical attention to the species of fiction which it describes in order to a generalizing of its peculiarities. It first came into general use in the latter half of the seventeenth century and the early years of the eighteenth; and naturally, was marked from birth with that shade of disapproval which has been noticed in popular usage. The feature that struck the critics most in the romances of the Middle Ages, and in that very different variety of romance which was cultivated during the seventeenth century—the prolix, sentimental fictions of La Calprenède, Scudéri, Gomberville, and D'Urfé—was the fantastic improbability of their adventures.

Hence the common acceptation of the word *romantic* in such phrases as "a romantic notion," "a romantic elopement," "an act of romantic generosity." The application of the adjective to scenery was somewhat later, and the abstract *romanticism* was, of course, very much later; as the literary movement, or the revolution in taste, which it entitles, was not enough developed to call for a name until the opening of the nineteenth century.

Indeed, it was never so compact, conscious, and definite a movement in England as in Germany and France; and its baptism doubtless came from abroad, from the polemical literature which attended the career of the German _romanticismus _and the French *romantisme*. While accepting provisionally Heine's definition, it will be useful to examine some of the wider meanings that have been attached to the words *classic* and *romantic*, and some of the analyses that have been attempted of the qualities that make one work of art classical and another romantic.

Walter Pater took them to indicate opposite tendencies or elements which are present in varying proportions in all good art. It is the essential function of classical art and literature, he thought, to take care of the qualities of measure, purity, temperance. "What is classical comes to us out of the cool and quiet of other times, as a measure of what a long experience has shown us will, at least, never displease us. And in the classical literature of Greece and Rome, as in the classics of the last century, the essentially classical element is that quality of order in beauty which they possess, indeed, in a pre-eminent degree." "The charm, then, of what is classical in art or literature is that of the well-known tale, to which we can nevertheless listen over and over again, because it is told so well. To the absolute beauty of its form is added the accidental, tranquil charm of familiarity." On the other hand, he defines the romantic characteristics in art as consisting in "the addition of strangeness to beauty"—a definition which recalls Bacon's saying, "There is no excellent beauty that hath not some strangeness in the proportion." "The desire of beauty," continues Pater, "being a fixed element in every artistic organization, it is the addition of curiosity to this desire of beauty that constitutes the romantic temper."

This critic, then, would not confine the terms *classic* and *classicism* to the literature of Greece and Rome and to modern works conceived in the same spirit, although he acknowledges that there are certain ages of the world in which the classical tradition predominates, *i.e.*, in which the respect for authority, the love of order and decorum, the disposition to follow rules and models, the acceptance of academic and conventional standards overbalance the desire for strangeness and novelty. Such epochs are, *e.g.*, the Augustan age of Rome, the *Siècle de Louis XIV*, in France, the times of Pope and Johnson in England.

Neither would he limit the word *romantic* to work conceived in the spirit of the Middle Ages. "The essential elements," he says, "of the romantic spirit are curiosity and the love of beauty; and it is as the accidental effect of these qualities only, that it seeks the Middle Ages; because in the overcharged atmosphere of the Middle Age there are unworked sources of romantic effect, of a strange beauty to be won by strong imagination out of things unlikely or remote." "The sense in which Scott is to be called a romantic writer is chiefly that, in opposition to the literary tradition of the last century, he loved strange adventure and sought it in the Middle Age."

Remarkably, here again the essayist is careful to explain that there are certain epochs which are predominately romantic. "Outbreaks of this spirit come naturally with particular periods: times when . . . men come to art and poetry with a deep thirst for intellectual excitement, after a long *ennui*." He instances, as periods naturally romantic, the time of the early Provençal troubadour poetry: the years following the Bourbon Restoration in France; and "the later Middle Age; so that the medieval poetry, centering in Dante, is often opposed to Greek or Roman poetry, as romantic to classical poetry." In Pater's use of the terms, then, classic and romantic do not describe particular literature, or particular periods in literary history, so much as certain counterbalancing qualities and tendencies which run through the literatures of all times and countries. There were romantic writings among the Greeks and Romans; there were classical writings in the Middle Ages; nay, there are classical and romantic traits in the same author.

If there is any poet who may safely be described as a classic, it is Sophocles; and yet Pater declares that the "Philoctetes" of Sophocles, if issued to-day, would be called romantic. And he points out—what indeed has been often pointed out—that the "Odyssey" is more romantic than the "Iliad:" is, in fact, rather a romance than a hero-epic. The adventures of the wandering Ulysses, the visit to the land of the lotus-eaters, the encounter with the Laestrygonians, the experiences in the cave of Polyphemus, if allowance be made for the difference in sentiments and manners, remind the reader constantly of the medieval *romans d'aventure*.

Pater quotes De Stendhal's saying that all good art was romantic in its day. "Romanticism," says De Stendhal, "is the art of presenting to the nations the literary works which, in the actual state of their habits and beliefs, are capable of giving them the greatest possible pleasure: classicism, on the contrary, presents them with what gave the greatest possible pleasure to their great grand-fathers"—a definition which is epigrammatic, if not convincing. De Stendhal (Henri Beyle) was a pioneer and a special pleader in the cause of French romanticism, and, in his use of the terms, romanticism stands for progress, liberty, originality, and the spirit of the future; classicism, for conservatism, authority, imitation, the spirit of the past. According to him, every good piece of romantic art is a classic in the making. Decried by the classicists of to-day, for its failure to observe traditions, it will be used by the classicists of the future as a pattern to which new artists must conform. It may be worth while to round out the conception of the term by considering a few other definitions of *romantic* which have been proposed.

Dr. F. H. Hedge, in an article in the *Atlantic Monthly* (March, 1886), inquired, "What do we mean by romantic?" Goethe, he says, characterized the difference between classic and romantic "as equivalent to [that between] healthy and morbid. Schiller proposed 'naïve and sentimental.' The greater part [of the German critics] regarded it as identical with the difference between ancient and modern, which was partly true, but explained nothing. None of the definitions given could be accepted as quite satisfactory."

Dr. Hedge writes "The essence of romance," "is mystery"; and he enforces the point by noting the application of the word to scenery. "The woody dell, the leafy glen, the forest path which leads, one knows not whither, are romantic: the public highway is not." "The winding secret brook . . . is romantic, as compared with the broad river." "Moonlight is romantic, as contrasted with daylight." He attributes this fondness for the mysterious to "the influence of the Christian religion, which deepened immensely the mystery of life, suggesting something beyond and behind the world of sense."

Remarkably, his charm of wonder or mystery is perhaps only another name for that "strangeness added to beauty" which Pater takes to be the distinguishing feature of romantic art. Further, he asserts that "the essence of romanticism is aspiration." Much might be said in defense of this position. It has often been pointed out, *e.g.*, that a Gothic cathedral expresses aspiration, and a Greek temple satisfied completeness. Indeed if we agree that, in a general way, the classic is equivalent to the antique, and the romantic to the medieval, it will be strange if we do not discover many differences between the two that can hardly be covered by any single phrase. Dr. Hedge himself enumerates several qualities of romantic art which it would be difficult to bring under his essential and defining category of wonder or aspiration.

Thus he announces that "the peculiarity of the classic style is reserve, self-suppression of the writer"; while "the romantic is self-reflecting." "Clear, unimpassioned, impartial presentation of the subject . . . is the prominent feature of the classic style. The modern writer gives you not so much the things themselves as his impression of them." Here then is the familiar critical distinction between the objective and subjective methods—Schiller's *naiv and sentimentalisch*—applied as a criterion of classic and romantic style.

This contrast the essayist develops at some length, dwelling upon "the cold reserve and colorless simplicity of the classic style, where the medium is lost in the object"; and "on the other hand, the inwardness, the sentimental intensity, the subjective coloring of the romantic style." A further distinguishing mark of the romantic spirit, mentioned by Dr. Hedge in common with many other critics, is the indefiniteness or incompleteness of its creations. This is a consequence, of course, of its sense of mystery and aspiration. Schopenbauer said that music was the characteristic modern art, because of its subjective, indefinite character.

Pursuing this line of thought, Dr. Hedge affirms that "romantic relates to classic somewhat as music relates to plastic art. . . It [music] presents no finished ideal, but suggests ideals beyond the capacity of canvas or stone. Plastic art acts on the intellect, music on the feelings; the one affects us by what it presents, the other by what it suggests. This, it seems to me, is essentially the difference between classic and romantic poetry"; and he names Homer and Milton as examples of the former, and Scott and Shelley of the latter school. Here then we have a third criterion proposed for determining the essential *differentia* of romantic art. First it was mystery, then aspiration; now it is the appeal to the emotions by the method of suggestion. And yet there is, perhaps, no inconsistency on the critic's part in this continual shifting of his ground.

He is apparently presenting different facets of the same truth; he means one thing by this mystery, aspiration, indefiniteness, incompleteness, emotion suggestiveness: that quality or effect which we all feel to be present in romantic and absent from classic work, but which we find it hard to describe by any single term. It is open to any analyst of our critical vocabulary to draw out the fullest meanings that he can, from such pairs of related words as classic and romantic, fancy and imagination, wit and humor, reason and understanding, passion and sentiment. Let us, for instance, develop briefly this proposition that the ideal of classic art is completeness and the ideal of romantic art indefiniteness, or suggestiveness.

A.W. Schlegel had already made use of two of the arts of design, to illustrate the distinction between classic and romantic, just as Hedge uses plastic art and music. I refer to Schlegel's famous saying that the genius of the antique drama was statuesque, and that of the romantic drama picturesque. A Greek temple, statue, or poem has no imperfection and offers no further promise, indicates nothing beyond what it expresses. It fills the sense, it leaves nothing to the imagination.

It stands correct, symmetric, sharp in outline, in the clear light of day. There is nothing more to be done to it; there is no concealment about it. But in romantic art there is seldom this completeness. The workman lingers, he would fain add another touch, his ideal eludes him. Is a Gothic cathedral ever really finished? Is "Faust" finished? Is "Hamlet" explained? The modern spirit is mystical; its architecture, painting, poetry employ shadow to produce their highest effects: shadow and color rather than contour.

On the Greek heroic stage there were a few figures, two or three at most, grouped like statuary and thrown out in bold relief at the apex of the scene: in Greek architecture a few clean, simple lines: in Greek poetry clear conceptions easily expressible in language and mostly describable in sensuous images. The modern theater is crowded with figures and colors, and the distance recedes in the middle of the scene. This love of perspective is repeated in cathedral aisles, the love of color in cathedral windows, and obscurity hovers in the shadows of the vault. In our poetry, in our religion these twilight thoughts prevail. We seek no completeness here. What is beyond, what is inexpressible attracts us. Hence the greater spirituality of romantic literature, its deeper emotion, its more passionate tenderness.

But hence likewise its sentimentality, its melancholy and, in particular, the morbid fascination which the thought of death has had for the Gothic mind. The classic nations concentrated their attention on life and light, and spent few thoughts upon darkness and the tomb. Death was to them neither sacred nor beautiful. Their decent rites of sepulture or cremation seem designed to hide its deformities rather than to prolong its reminders. The presence of the corpse was pollution. No Greek could have conceived such a book as the "Hydriotaphia" or the "Anatomy of Melancholy."

It is observable that Hedge is at one with Pater, in desiring some more philosophical statement of the difference between classic and romantic than the common one which makes it simply the difference between the antique and the medieval. He says: "It must not be supposed that ancient and classic, on one side, and modern and romantic, on the other, are inseparably one; so that nothing approaching to romantic shall be found in any Greek or Roman author, nor any classic page in the literature of modern Europe. .

. The literary line of demarcation is not identical with the chronological one."

And just as Pater says that the Odyssey is more romantic than the Iliad, so Dr. Hedge says that "the story of Cupid and Psyche, in the 'Golden Ass' of Apuleius, is as much a romance as any composition of the seventeenth or eighteenth century." Medievalism he regards as merely an accident of romance: Scott, as most romantic in his themes, but Byron, in his mood. Sidney Colvin denies that "a predilection for classic subjects . . . can make a writer that which we understand by the word classical as distinguished from that which we understand by the word romantic. The distinction lies deeper, and is a distinction much less of subject than of treatment. . . In classical writing every idea is called up to the mind as nakedly as possible, and at the same time as distinctly; it is exhibited in white light, and left to produce its effect by its own unaided power. In romantic writing, on the other hand, all objects are exhibited, as it were, through a colored and iridescent atmosphere.

Round about every central idea the romantic writer summons up a cloud of accessory and subordinate ideas for the sake of enhancing its effect, if at the risk of confusing its outlines. The temper, again, of the romantic writer is one of excitement, while the temper of the classical writer is one of self-possession. . . On the one hand there is calm, on the other hand enthusiasm. The virtues of the one style are strength of grasp, with clearness and justice of presentment; the virtues of the other style are glow of the spirit, with magic and richness of suggestion."

Colvin then goes on to enforce and illustrate this contrast between the "accurate and firm definition of things" in classical writers and the "thrilling vagueness and uncertainty," the tremulous, coruscating, vibrating or colored light—the "halo"—with which the romantic writer invests his theme. "The romantic manner, . . . with its thrilling uncertainties and its rich suggestions, may be more attractive than the classic manner, with its composed and measured preciseness of statement. . . But on the other hand the romantic manner lends itself, as the true classical does not, to inferior work. Second-rate conceptions excitedly and approximately put into words derive from it an illusive attraction which may make them for a time, and with all but the coolest judges, pass as first-rate.

Whereas about true classical writing there can be no illusion. It presents to us conceptions calmly realized in words that exactly define them, conceptions depending for their attraction, not on their halo, but on themselves." As examples of these contrasting styles, Colvin puts side by side passages from "The Ancient Mariner" and Keats' "Ode to a Nightingale," with passages, treating similar themes, from Landor's "Gebir" and "Imaginary Conversations." The contrast might be even more clearly established by a study of such a piece as Keats' "Ode on a Grecian Urn," where the romantic form is applied to classical content; or by a comparison of Tennyson's "Ulysses" and "The Lotus Eaters," in which Homeric subjects are treated respectively in the classic and the romantic manner. Alfred de Musset, himself in early life a prominent figure among the French romanticists, wrote some capital satire upon the baffling and contradictory definitions of the word *romantisme* that were current in the third and fourth decades of this century. Two worthy provincials write from the little town of La Ferté-sous-Jouarre to the editor of the "Revue des Deux Mondes," appealing to him to tell them what romanticism means.

For two years Dupuis and his friend Cotonet had supposed that the term applied only to the theater, and signified the disregard of the unities. "Shakspeare, for example makes people travel from Rome to London, and from Athens to Alexandria in a quarter of an hour. His heroes live ten or twenty years between two acts. His heroines, angels of virtue during a whole scene, have only to pass into the *coulisses*, to reappear as wives, adulteresses, widows, and grandmothers.

There, we said to ourselves, is the romantic. Contrariwise, Sophocles makes Oedipus sit on a rock, even at the cost of great personal inconvenience, from the very beginning of his tragedy. All the characters come there to find him, one after the other. Perhaps he stands up occasionally, though I doubt it; unless, it may be, out of respect for Theseus, who, during the entire play, obligingly walks on the highway, coming in or going out continually. . . There, we said to ourselves, is the classic." But about 1828, continues the letter, "we learned that there were romantic poetry and classical poetry, romantic novels and classical novels, romantic odes and classical odes; nay, a single line, my dear sir, a sole and solitary line of verse might be romantic or classic, according as the humor took it. When we received this intelligence, we could not close our eyes all night.

Two years of peaceful conviction had vanished like a dream. All our ideas were turned topsy-turvy; for it the rules of Aristotle were no longer the line of demarcation which separated the literary camps, where was one to find himself, and what was he to depend upon? How was one to know, in reading a book, which school it belonged to? . . . Luckily in the same year there appeared a famous preface, which we devoured straightway. . . This said very distinctly that romanticism was nothing else than the alliance of the playful and the serious, of the grotesque and the terrible, of the jocose and the horrible, or in other words, if you prefer, of comedy and tragedy." This definition the anxious inquirers accepted for the space of a year, until it was borne in upon them that Aristophanes—not to speak of other ancients—had mixed tragedy and comedy in his drama.

Once again the friends were plunged in darkness, and their perplexity was deepened when they were taking a walk one evening and overheard a remark made by the niece of the *sous-prefet*. This young lady had fallen in love with English ways, as was—somewhat strangely—evidenced by her wearing a green veil, orange-colored gloves, and silver-rimmed spectacles. As she passed the promenaders, she turned to look at a water-mill near the ford, where there were bags of grain, geese, and an ox in harness, and she exclaimed to her governess, "*Voilà un site romantique.*" This mysterious sentence roused the flagging curiosity of MM. Dupuis and Contonet, and they renewed their investigations. A passage in a newspaper led them to believe for a time that romanticism was the imitation of the Germans, with, perhaps, the addition of the English and Spanish.

Then they were tempted to fancy that it might be merely a matter of literary form, possibly this *vers brisé* (run-over lines, *enjambement*) that they are making so much noise about. "From 1830 to 1831 we were persuaded that romanticism was the historic style (*genre historique*) or, if you please, this mania which has lately seized our authors for calling the characters of their novels and melodramas Charlemagne, Francis I., or Henry IV., instead of Amadis, Oronte, or saint-Albin.

From 1831 to the year following we thought it was the *genre intime,* about which there was much talk. But with all the pains that we took we never could discover what the *genre intime* was. The 'intimate' novels are just like the others. They are in two volume octavo, with a great deal of margin. . . They have yellow covers and they cost fifteen francs." From 1832 to 1833 they conjectured that romanticism might be a system of philosophy and political economy. From 1833 to 1834 they believed that it consisted in not shaving one's self, and in wearing a waistcoat with wide facings very much starched. At last they bethink themselves of a certain lawyer's clerk, who had first imported these literary disputes into the village, in 1824. To him, they expose their difficulties and ask for an answer to the question, What is romanticism? After a long conversation, they receive this final definition. "Romanticism, my dear sir! No, of a surety, it is neither the disregard of the unities, nor the alliance of the comic and tragic, nor anything in the world expressible by words. In vain you grasp the butterfly's wing; the dust which gives it its color is left upon your fingers.

Romanticism is the star that weeps, it is the wind that wails, it is the night that shudders, the bird that flies and the flower that breathes perfume: it is the sudden gush, the ecstasy grown faint, the cistern beneath the palms, rosy hope with her thousand loves, the angel and the pearl, the white robe of the willows. It is the infinite and the starry," etc., etc. Then M. Ducoudray, a magistrate of the department, gives his theory of romanticism, which he considers to be an effect of the religious and political reaction under the restored Bourbon monarchy of Louis XVIII, and Charles X. "The mania for ballads, arriving from Germany, met the legitimist poetry one fine day at Ladvocat's bookshop; and the two of them, pickax in hand, went at nightfall to a churchyard, to dig up the Middle Ages." The taste for medievalism, M. Ducoudray adds, has survived the revolution of 1830, and romanticism has even entered into the service of liberty and progress, where it is a manifest anachronism, "employing the style of Ronsard to celebrate railroads, and imitating Dante when it chants the praises of Washington and Lafayette."

Dupuis was tempted to embrace M. Ducoudray's explanation, but Cotonet was not satisfied. He shut himself in, for four months, at the end of which he announced his discovery that the true and only difference between the classic and the romantic is that the latter uses a good many adjectives. He illustrates his principle by giving passages from "Paul and Virginia" and the "Portuguese Letters," written in the romantic style. Thus Musset pricks a critical bubble with the point of his satire; and yet the bubble declines to vanish. There must really be some more substantial difference than this between classic and romantic, for the terms persist and are found useful. It may be true that the romantic temper, being subjective and excited, tends to an excess in adjectives; the adjective being that part of speech which attributes qualities, and is therefore most freely used by emotional persons. Still it would be possible to cut out all the adjectives, not strictly necessary, from one of Tieck's *Märchen* without in the slightest degree disturbing its romantic character.

It remains to add that romanticism is a word which faces in two directions. It is now opposed to realism, as it was once opposed to classicism. As, in one way, its freedom and lawlessness, its love of novelty, experiment, "strangeness added to beauty," contrast with the classical respect for rules, models, formulae, precedents, conventions; so, in another way, its discontent with things as they are, its idealism, aspiration, mysticism contrast with the realist's conscientious adherence to fact.

3
The Augustans

In common parlance the Augastan Age denotes a period of literary excellence, and refers back to the heyday of classical writing during the reign of the Roman Emperor Augustus. Common literary concerns, especially among the poets included: the development of an elegant, well-turned style; the pursuit of fluency, precision of expression and a dislike of cant or slang, the observation of decorum; an the cultivation of good taste and the refinement of manner.

As is mentioned in preceding chapters, Romantic Movement in England was a part of the general European reaction against the spirit of the eighteenth century. This began somewhat earlier in England than in Germany, and very much earlier than in France, where literacy conservatism went strangely hand in hand with political radicalism. In England the reaction was at first gradual, timid, and unconscious. It did not reach importance until the seventh decade of the century, and culminated only in the early years of the nineteenth century. The medieval revival was only an incident—though a leading incident—of this movement; but it is the side of it with which the present work will mainly deal.

Heine's definition—of romanticism, as the reproduction in modern art and literature of the life of the Middle Ages, it should be explained that the expression, "Middle Ages," is to be taken here in a liberal sense. Contributions to romantic literature such as Macpherson's "Ossian," Collins' "Ode on the Superstitions of the Scottish Highlands," and Gray's translations form the Welsh and the Norse, relate to periods which antedate that era of Christian chivalry and feudalism, extending roughly from the eleventh century to the fifteenth, to which the term, "Middle Ages," more strictly applies.

In fact, the same thing is true of the ground-work, at least, of ancient hero-epics like "Beowulf" and the "Nibelungen Lied," of the Icelandic "Sagas," and of similar products of old heathen Europe which have come down in the shape of mythologies, popular superstitions, usages, rites, songs, and traditions. These began to fall under the notice of scholars about the middle of the last century and made a deep impression upon contemporary letters.

It is pertinent to note that, the influence of the Middle Age proper prolonged itself beyond the exact close of the medieval period, which it is customary to date from the fall of Constantinople in 1453. The great romantic poets of Italy, Boiardo, Ariosto, Tasso, wrote in the full flush of the pagan revival and made free use of the Greek and Roman mythologies and the fables of Homer, Vergil, and Ovid; and yet their work is hardly to be described as classical. Nor is the work of their English disciples, Spenser and Sidney; while the entire Spanish and English drama of the sixteenth and seventeenth centuries is romantic.

Calderon is romantic; Shakspeare and Fletcher are romantic. If we agree to regard medieval literature, then, as comprising all the early literature of Europe which drew its inspiration from other than Greek-Latin sources, we shall do no great violence to the usual critical employment of the word. In fact, early literature, in order to exclude such writings as are wholly modern, like *"Robinson Crusoe,"* or *"Gulliver's Travels,"* or Fielding's novels, which are neither classic nor romantic, but are the original creation of our own time. With works like these, though they are perhaps the most characteristic output of the eighteenth century, our inquiries are not concerned.

It hardly needs to be said that the reproduction, or imitation, of mediaeval life by the eighteenth- and nineteenth-century romanticists, contains a large admixture of modern thought and feeling. The brilliant pictures of feudal society in the romances of Scott and Fouqué give no faithful image of that society, even when they are carefully correct in all ascertainable historical details. They give rather the impression left upon an alien mind by the quaint, picturesque features of a way of life which seemed neither quaint nor picturesque to the men who lived it, but only to the man who turns to it for relief form the prosaic, or at least familiar, conditions of the modern world.

The offspring of the modern imagination, acting upon medieval material, may be a perfectly legitimate, though not an original, form of art. It may even have a novel charm of its own, unlike either parent, but like Euphorion, child of Faust by Helen of Troy, a blend of Hellas and the Middle Age. Scott's verse tales are better poetry than the English metrical romances of the thirteenth and fourteenth centuries. Tennyson has given a more perfect shape to the Arthurian legends than Sir Thomas Malory, their compiler, or Walter Map and Chrestien de Troyes, their possible inventors.

But, of course, to study the Middle Ages, as it really was, one must go not to Tennyson and Scott, but to the "Chanson de Roland," and the "Divine Comedy," and the "Romaunt of the Rose," and the chronicles of Villehardouin, Joinville, and Froissart.

The Middle Ages was not, at all points, romantic: it is the modern romanticist who makes, or finds, it so. He sees its strange, vivid peculiarities under the glamour of distance. Chaucer's temper, for instance, was by no means romantic. This "good sense" which Dryden mentions as his prominent trait; that "low tone" which Lowell praises in him, and which keeps him close to the common ground of experience, pervade his greatest work, the "Canterbury Tales," with an insistent realism.

It is true that Chaucer shared the beliefs and influences of his time and was a follower of its literary fashions. In his version of the *"Romaunt of the Rose,"* his imitations of Machault, and his early work in general he used the mediaeval machinery of allegory and dreams. In *"Troilus and Cresseide"* and the tale of *"Palamon and Arcite,"* he carries romantic love and knightly honor to a higher pitch than his model, Boccaccio. But the shrewdly practical Pandarus of the former poem—a character almost wholly of Chaucer's creation—is the very embodiment of the anti-romantic attitude, and a remarkable anticipation of Sancho Panza; while the "Rime of Sir Thopas" is a distinct burlesque of the fantastic chivalry romances. Chaucer's pages are picturesque with tournament, hunting parties, baronial feasts, miracles of saints, feats of magic; but they are solid, as well, with the everyday life of fourteenth-century England.

They have the naïveté and garrulity which are marks of mediaeval work, but not the quaintness and grotesquerie which are held to be marks of romantic work. Not archaic speech, but a certain mental twist constitutes quaintness. Herbert and Fuller are quaint; Blake is grotesque; Donne and Charles Lamb are willfully quaint, subtle, and paradoxical. But Chaucer is always straight-grained, broad, and natural.

Even Dante, the poet of the Catholic Middle Ages; Dante, the mystic, the idealist, with his intense spirituality and his passion for symbolism, has been sometimes called classic, by virtue of the powerful construction of his great poem, and his scholastic rigidity of method. The relation between modern romanticizing literature and the real literature of the Middle Ages, is something like that between the literature of the renaissance and the ancient literatures of Greece and Rome.

But there is this difference, that, while the renaissance writers fell short of their pattern, the modern schools of romance have outgone their masters—not perhaps in the intellectual—but certainly in the artistic value of their product. Mediaeval literature, wonderful and stimulating as a whole and beautiful here and there in details of execution, affords few models of technical perfection. The civilization which it reflected, though higher in its possibilities than the classic civilization, had not yet arrived at an equal grade of development, was inferior in intelligence and the natured results of long culture. The epithets of Gothic ignorance, rudeness, and barbarism, which the eighteenth-century critics applied so freely to all the issue of the so-called dark ages, were not entirely without justification. Dante is almost the only strictly mediaeval poet in whose work the form seems adequate to the content; for Boccaccio and Petrarca stand already on the sill of the renaissance. In the arts of design the case was partly reversed. If the artists of the renaissance did not equal the Greeks in sculpture and architecture, they probably excelled them in painting. On the other hand, the restorers of Gothic have never quite learned the secret of the mediaeval builders.

However, if the analogy is not pushed too far, the romantic revival may be regarded as a faint counterpart, the fragments of a half-forgotten civilization were pieced together; Greek manuscripts sought out, cleaned, edited, and printed: statues, coins, vases dug up and ranged in museums: debris cleared away from temples, amphitheaters, basilicas; till gradually the complete image of the antique world grew forth in august beauty, kindling an excitement of mind to which there are few parallels in history; so, in the eighteenth century, the despised ages of monkery, feudalism, and superstition began to reassert their claims upon the imagination. Ruined castles and abbeys, coats of mail, illuminated missals, manuscript romances, black-letter ballads, old tapestries, and wood carvings acquired a new value.

Antiquaries and virtuosos first, and then poets and romancers, reconstructed in turn an image of medieval society. True, the later movement was much the weaker of the two. No such fissure yawned between modern times and the Middle Ages as had been opened between the ancient world and the Middle Ages by the ruin of the Roman state and by the barbarian migrations. Nor had ten centuries of rubbish accumulated over the remains of mediaeval culture. In 1700 the Middle Ages were not yet so very remote.

The nations and languages of Europe continued in nearly the same limits which had bounded them two centuries before. The progress in the sciences and mechanic arts, the discovery and colonizing of America, the invention of printing and gunpowder, and the Protestant reformation had indeed drawn deep lines between modern and mediaeval life. Christianity, however, formed a connecting link, though, in Protestant countries, the continuity between the earlier and later forms of the religion had been interrupted.

One has but to compare the list of the pilgrims whom Chaucer met at the Tabard, with the company that Captain Sentry or Peregrine Pickle would be likely to encounter at a suburban inn, to see how the face of English society had changed between 1400 and 1700. What has become of the knight, the prioress, the sumner, the monk, pardoner, squire, alchemist, friar; and where can they or their equivalents be found in all England?

It would be unphilosophical to consider it as a merely aesthetic affair, and to lose sight altogether of its deeper springs in the religious and ethical currents of the time. For it was, in part, a return of warmth and color into English letters; and that was only a symptom of the return of warmth and color—that is, of emotion and imagination—into English life and thought: into the Church, into politics, into philosophy.

Romanticism, which sought to evoke from the past a

beauty that it found wanting in the present, was but one phase of that revolt against the coldness and spiritual deadness of the first half of the eighteenth century which had other sides in the idealism of Berkeley, in the Methodist and Evangelical revival led by Wesley and Whitefield, and in the sentimentalism which manifested itself in the writings of Richardson and Sterne. Corresponding to these on the Continent were German pietism, the transcendental philosophy of Kant and his continuators, and the emotional excesses of works like Rousseau's *"Nouvelle Héloise"* and Goethe's *"Sorrows of Werther."*

It is pertinent to note that Romanticism was something more, then, than a new literary mode; a taste cultivated by dilettante virtuosos, like Horace Walpole, college recluses like Gray, and antiquarian scholars like Joseph and Thomas Warton. It was the effort of the poetic imagination to create for itself a richer environment; but it was also, in its deeper significance, a reaching out of the human spirit after a more ideal type of religion and ethics than it could find in the official churchmanship and the formal morality of the time.

Leslie Stephen points out the connection between the three currents of tendency known as sentimentalism, romanticism, and naturalism. He explains, to be sure, that the first English sentimentalists, such as Richardson and Sterne, were anything but romantic. "A more modern sentimentalist would probably express his feelings by describing some past state of society. He would paint some ideal society in mediaeval times and revive the holy monk and the humble nun for our edification." He attributes the subsequent interest in the Middle Ages to the progress made in historical inquiries during the last half of the eighteenth century, and to the consequent growth of antiquarianism. "Men like Malone and Stevens were beginning those painful researches which have accumulated a whole literature upon the scanty records of our early dramatists.

Gray, the most learned of poets, had vaguely designed a history of English poetry, and the design was executed with great industry by Thomas Warton. His brother Joseph ventured to uphold the then paradoxical thesis that Spenser was as great a man as Pope. Everywhere a new interest was awakening in the minuter details of the past." At first, Mr. Stephen says, the result of these inquiries was "an unreasonable contempt for the past.

The modern philosopher, who could spin all knowledge out of his own brain; the skeptic, who had exploded the ancient dogma; or the free-thinker of any shade, who rejoiced in the destruction of ecclesiastical tyranny, gloried in his conscious superiority to his forefathers. Whatever was old was absurd; and Gothic—an epithet applied to all medieval art, philosophy, or social order—became a simple term of contempt." But an antiquarian is naturally a conservative, and men soon began to love the times whose peculiarities they were so diligently studying. Men of imaginative minds promptly made the discovery that a new source of pleasure might be derived from these dry records. . . The 'return to nature' expresses a sentiment which underlies . . . both the sentimental and romantic movements. . . To return to nature is, in one sense, to find a new expression for emotions which have been repressed by existing conventions; or, in another, to return to some simpler social order which had not yet suffered from those conventions.

The artificiality attributed to the eighteenth century seems to mean that men were content to regulate their thoughts and lives by rules not traceable to first principles, but dependent upon a set of special and exceptional conditions. . . To get out of the ruts, or cast off the obsolete shackles, two methods might be adopted. The intellectual horizon might be widened by including a greater number of ages and countries; or men might try to fall back upon the thoughts and emotions common to all races, and so cast off the superficial incrustation. The first method, that of the romanticists, aims at increasing our knowledge: the second, that of the naturalistic school, at basing our philosophy on deeper principles.

The classic, or pseudo-classic, period of English literature lasted from the middle of the seventeenth till the end of the eighteenth century. Inasmuch as the romantic revival was a protest against this reigning mode, it becomes necessary to inquire a little more closely what we mean when we say that the time of Queen Anne and the first two Georges was English Augustan or classical age.

If the "Dunciad," and the "Essay on Man," are classical, what is Keats' "Hyperion"? And with what propriety can we bring under a common rubric things so far asunder as Prior's "Carmen Seculare" and Tennyson's "Ulysses," or as Gay's "Trivia" and Swinburne's "Atalanta in Calydon"? Evidently the Queen Anne writers took hold of the antique by a different side from our nineteenth-century poets. Their classicism was of a special type. It was, as has been often pointed out, more Latin than Greek, and more French than Latin It was, as has likewise been said, "a classicism in red heels and a periwig." Victor Hugo speaks of "cette poésie fardée, mouchetée, poudrée, du dix-huitième siècle, cette litèrature à paniers, à pompons et à falbalas." The costumes of Watteau contrast with the simple folds of Greek drapery very much as the "Rape of the Lock," contrasts with the Iliad, or one of Pope's pastorals with an idyl of Theocritus.

Gentlemen wore powdered wigs instead of their own hair, and the power and the wig both got into their writing. Perruque was the nickname applied to the classicists by the French romanticists of Hugo's generation, who wore their hair long and flowing—cheveaux mérovigiennes—and affected an outré freedom in the cut and color of their clothes. Similarly the Byronic collar became, all over Europe, the symbol of daring independence in matters of taste and opinion. Its careless roll, which left the throat exposed, seemed to assist the liberty of nature against cramping conventions.

The leading Queen Anne writers are so well known that a somewhat general description of the literary situation in England at the time of Pope's death (1744) will serve as an answer to the question, how was the eighteenth century classical. It was remarked by Thomas Warton that, at the first revival of letters in the sixteenth century, our authors were more struck by the marvelous fables and inventions of ancient poets than by the justness of their conceptions and the purity of their style. In other words, the men of the renaissance apprehended the ancient literature as poets: the men of the Éclaircissement apprehended them as critics. In Elizabeth's day the new learning stimulated English genius to creative activity. In royal progresses, court masques, Lord Mayors' shows, and public pageants of all kinds, mythology ran mad. "Every procession was a pantheon." But the poets were not careful to keep the two worlds of pagan antiquity and mediaeval Christianity distinct. The art of the renaissance was the flower of a double root, and the artists used their complex stuff naïvely. The "Faërie Queene" is the typical work of the English renaissance; there hamadryads, satyrs, and river gods mingle unblushingly with knights, dragons, sorcerers, hermits, and personified vices and virtues. The "machinery" of Homer and Vergil—the "machinery" of the "Seven Champions of Christendom" and the "Roman de la Rose"! This was not shocking to Spenser's contemporaries, but it seemed quite shocking to classical critics a century later. Even Milton, the greatest scholar among English poets, but whose imagination was a strong agent, holding strange elements in solution, incurred their censure for bringing Saint Peter and the sea-nymphs into dangerous juxtaposition in "Lycidas."

But by the middle of the seventeenth century the renaissance schools of poetry had become effete in all European countries. They had run into extravagances of style, into a vicious manner known in Spain as Gongorism, in Italy as Marinism, and in England best exhibited in the verse of Donne and Cowley and the rest of the group whom Dr. Johnson called the metaphysical poets, and whose Gothicism of taste Addison ridiculed in his Spectator papers on true and false wit. It was France that led the reform against this fashion. Malherbe and Boileau insisted upon the need of discarding tawdry ornaments of style and cultivating simplicity, clearness, propriety, decorum, moderation; above all, good sense. The new Academy, founded to guard the purity of the French language, lent its weight to the precepts of the critics, who applied the rules of Aristotle, as commented by Longinus and Horace, to modern conditions. The appearance of a number of admirable writers—Corneille, Molière, Racine, Bossuet, La Fontaine, La Bruyère—simultaneously with this critical movement, gave an authority to the new French literature which enabled it to impose its principles upon England and Germany for over a century. For the creative literature of France conformed its practice, in the main, to the theory of French criticism; though not, in the case of Regnier, without open defiance. This authority was re-enforced by the political glories and social éclat of the siècle de Louis Quatorze

It happened that at this time the Stuart court was in exile, and in the train of Henrietta Maria at Paris, or scattered elsewhere through France, were many royalist men of letters, Etherege, Waller, Cowley, and others, who brought back with them to England in 1660 an acquaintance with this new French literature and a belief in its aesthetic code. That French influence would have spread into England without the aid of these political accidents is doubtless true, as it is also true that a reform of English versification and poetic style would have worked itself out upon native lines independent of foreign example, and even had there been so such thing as French literature. Gosse has pointed out couplets of Waller, written as early as 1623, which have the formal precision of Pope's; and the famous passage about the Thames in Denham's "Cooper's Hill" (1642) anticipates the best performance of Augustan verse:

> "O could I flow like thee, and make thy stream
> My great example, as it is my theme!
> Though deep, yet clear, though gentle, yet not dull,
> Strong without rage, without o'erflowing full."

However, as to the general fact of the powerful impact of French upon English literary fashions, in the latter half of the seventeenth century, there can be no dispute.

This change of style was symptomatic of a corresponding change in the national temper. It was the mission of the eighteenth century to assert the universality of law and, at the same time, the sufficiency of the reason to discover the laws, which govern in every province: a service which we now, perhaps, undervalue in our impatience with the formalism which was its outward sign. Hence its dislike of irregularity in art and irrationality in religion. England, in particular, was tired of unchartered freedom, of spiritual as well as of literary anarchy.

The religious tension of the Commonwealth period had relaxed—men cannot be always at the heroic pitch—and theological disputes had issued in indifference and a skepticism which took the form of deism, or "natural religion." But the deists were felt to be a nuisance. They were unsettling opinions and disturbing that decent conformity with generally received beliefs which it is the part of a good citizen to maintain.

Addison instructs his readers that, in the absence of certainty, it is the part of a prudent man to choose the safe side and make friends with God. The freethinking Chesterfield tells his son that the profession of atheism is ill-bred. De Foe, Swift, Richardson, Fielding, Johnson all attack infidelity. "Conform! Conform!" said in effect the most authoritative writers of the century. "Be sensible: go to church: pay your rates: don't be a vulgar deist—a fellow like Toland who is poor and has no social position. But, on the other hand, you need not be a fanatic or superstitious, or an enthusiast. Above all, pas de zèle!"

Leslie Stephen says, "Theology, for the most part, almost as deistical as the deists. A hatred for enthusiasm was as strongly impressed upon the whole character of contemporary thought as a hatred of skepticism. . . A good common-sense religion should be taken for granted and no questions asked. . . With Shakspeare, or Sir Thomas Browne, or Jeremy Taylor, or Milton, man is contemplated in his relations to the universe; he is in presence of eternity and infinity; life is a brief drama; heaven and hell are behind the veil of phenomena; at every step our friends vanish into the abyss of ever present mystery. To all such thoughts the writers of the eighteenth century seemed to close their eyes as resolutely as possible. . . The absence of any deeper speculative ground makes the immediate practical questions of life all the more interesting. We know not what we are, nor whither we are going, nor whence we come; but we can, by the help of common sense, discover a sufficient share of moral maxims for our guidance in life. . . Knowledge of human nature, as it actually presented itself in the shifting scene before them, and a vivid appreciation of the importance of the moral law, are the staple of the best literature of the time."

The God of the deists was, in truth, hardly more impersonal than the abstraction worshipped by the orthodox—the "Great Being" of Addison's essays, the "Great First Cause" of Pope's "Universal Prayer," invoked indifferently as "Jehovah, Jove, or Lord." Dryden and Pope were professed Catholics, but there is nothing to distinguish their so-called sacred poetry from that of their Protestant contemporaries. Contrast the mere polemics of "The Hind and the Panther" with really Catholic poems like Southwell's "Burning Babe" and Crashaw's "Flaming Heart," or even with Newman's "Dream of Gerontius." In his "Essay on

Man," Pope versified, without well understanding, the optimistic deism of Leibnitz, as expounded by Shaftesbury and Bolingbroke. The Anglican Church itself was in a strange condition, when Jonathan Swift, a dean and would-be bishop, came to its defense with his "Tale of a Tub" and his ironical "Argument against the Abolition of Christianity."

Among the Queen Anne wits Addison was the man of most genuine religious feeling. He is always reverent, and "the feeling infinite" stirs faintly in one or two of his hymns. But, in general, his religion is of the rationalizing type, a religion of common sense, a belief resting upon logical deductions, a system of ethics in which the supernatural is reduced to the lowest terms, and from which the glooms and fervors of a deep spiritual experience are almost entirely absent.

This "parson in a tie-wig" is constantly preaching against zeal, enthusiasm, superstition, mysticism, and recommending a moderate, cheerful, and reason religion. It is instructive to contrast his amused contempt for popular beliefs in ghosts, witches, dreams, prognostications, and the like, with the reawakened interest in folk lore evidenced by such a book as Scott's "Demonology and Witchcraft."

Queen Anne literature was classical, then, in its lack of those elements of mystery and aspiration which we have found described as of the essence of romanticism. It was emphatically a literature of this world. It ignored all vague emotion, the phenomena of subconsciousness, "the electric chain wherewith we are darkly bound," the shadow that rounds man's little life, and fixed its attention only upon what it could thoroughly comprehend. Thereby it escaped obscurity. The writings of the Augustans in both verse and prose are distinguished by a perfect clearness, but it is a clearness without subtlety or depth. They never try to express a thought, or to utter a feeling, that is not easily intelligible. The mysticism of Wordsworth, the incoherence of Shelley, the darkness of Browning—to take only modern instances—proceed, however, not from inferior art, but from the greater difficulty of finding expression for a very different order of ideas.

Again the literature of the Restoration and Queen Anne periods—which may be regarded as one, for present purposes—was classical, or at least unromantic, in its self-restraint, its objectivity, and its lack of curiosity; or, as a hostile criticism would put it, in its coldness of feeling, the tameness of its imagination, and its narrow and imperfect sense of beauty. It was a literature not simply of this world, but of the world, of the beau monde, high life, fashion, society, the court and the town, the salons, clubs, coffee-houses, assemblies, ombre-parties. It was social, urban, gregarious, intensely though not broadly human. It cared little for the country or outward nature, and nothing for the life of remote times and places. Its interest was centered upon civilization and upon that peculiarly artificial type of civilization which it found prevailing. It was as indifferent to Venice, Switzerland, the Alhambra, the Nile, the American forests, and the islands of the South Sea as it was to the Middle Ages and the manners of Scotch Highlanders. The sensitiveness to the picturesque, the liking for local color and for whatever is striking, characteristic, and peculiarly national in foreign ways is a romantic note. The eighteenth century disliked "strangeness added to beauty"; it disapproved of anything original, exotic, tropical, bizarre for the same reason that it disapproved of mountains and Gothic architecture.

Professor Gates says that the work of English literature during the first quarter of the present century was "the rediscovery and vindication of the concrete. The special task of the eighteenth century had been to order, and to systematize, and to name; its favorite methods had been analysis and generalization. It asked for no new experience. . . The abstract, the typical, the general—these were everywhere exalted at the expense of the image, the specific experience, the vital fact." Classical tragedy, e.g., undertook to present only the universal, abstract, permanent truths of human character and passion. The impression of the mysterious East upon modern travelers and poets like Byron, Southey, De Quincey, Moore, Hugo, Ruckert, and Gérard de Nerval, has no counterpart in the eighteenth century. The Oriental allegory or moral apologue, as practiced by Addison in such papers as "The Vision of Mirza," and by Johnson in "Rasselas," is rather faintly colored and gets what color it has from the Old Testament. It is significant that the romantic Collins endeavored to give a novel turn to the decayed pastoral by writing a number of "Oriental Eclogues," in which dervishes and camel-drivers took the place of shepherds, but the experiment was not a lucky one. Milton had more of the East in his imagination than any of his successors. His "vulture on Imaus bred, whose snowy ridge the roving Tartar bounds"; his "plain of Sericana where Chinese drive their cany wagons light"; his "utmost Indian isle Taprobane," are touches of the picturesque which anticipate a more modern mood than Addison's.

"The difference," says Matthew Arnold, "between genuine poetry and the poetry of Dryden, Pope, and all their school is briefly this: their poetry is conceived and composed in their wits, genuine poetry is conceived and composed in the soul." The representative minds of the eighteenth century were such as Voltaire, the master of persiflage, destroying superstition with his souriere hideux; Gibbon, "the lord of irony," "sapping a solemn creed with solemn sneer"; and Hume, with his thorough-going philosophic skepticism, his dry Toryism, and cool contempt for "zeal" of any kind. The characteristic products of the era were satire, burlesque, and travesty: "Hudibras," "Absalom and Achitophel," "The Way of the World," "Gulliver's Travels" and "The Rape of the Lock." There is a whole literature of mockery: parodies like Prior's "Ballad on the Taking of Namur" and "The Country Mouse and the City Mouse"; Buckingham's "Rehearsal" and Swift's "Meditation on a Broomstick"; mock-heroics, like the "Dunciad" and "MacFlecknoe" and Garth's "Dispensary," and John Phillips' "Splendid Shilling" and

Addison's "Machinae Gesticulantes"; Prior's "Alma," a burlesque of philosophy; Gay's "Trivia" and "The Shepherd's Week," and "The Beggars' Opera"-a "Newgate pastoral"; "Town Eclogues" by Swift and Lady Montague and others.

Literature was a polished mirror in which the gay world saw its own grinning face. It threw back a most brilliant picture of the surface of society, showed manners but not the elementary passions of human nature. As a whole, it leaves an impression of hardness, shallowness, and levity. The polite cynicism of Congreve, the ferocious cynicism of Swift, the malice of Pope, the pleasantry of Addison, the early worldliness of Prior and Gay are seldom relieved by any touch of the ideal. The prose of the time was excellent, but the poetry was merely rhymed prose. The recent Queen Anne revival in architecture, dress, and bric-a-brac, the recrudescence of society verse in Dobson and others, is perhaps symptomatic of the fact that the present generation has entered upon a prosaic reaction against romantic excesses and we are finding our picturesque in that era of artifice which seemed so picturesque to our forerunners. The sedan chair, the blue china, the fan, farthingale, and powdered head dress have now got the "rime of age" and are seen in fascinating perspective, even as the mailed courser, the buff jerkin, the cowl, and the cloth-yard shaft were seen by the men of Scott's generation.

It must be remembered that, the eighteenth century was classical in its respect for authority. It desired to put itself under discipline, to follow the rules, to discover a formula of correctness in all the arts, to set up a tribunal of taste and establish canons of composition, to maintain standards, copy models and patterns, comply with conventions, and chastise lawlessness. In a word, its spirit was academic. Horace was its favorite master—not Horace of the Odes, but Horace of the Satires and Epistles, and especially Horace as interpreted by Boileau. The "Ars Poetica" had been englished by the Earl of Roscommon, and imitated by Boileau in his "L'Art Poetique," which became the parent of a numerous progeny in England; among others as "Essay on Satire" and an "Essay on Poetry," by the Earl of Mulgrave; an "Essay on Translated Verse" by the Earl of Roscommon, who, says Addison, "makes even rules a noble poetry".

In fact, the doctrine of Pope's essay is, in brief, follow Nature, and in order that you may follow nature, observe the rules, which are only "Nature methodized," and also imitate the ancients.

As such, Vergil when he started to compose the *Aeneid* may have seemed above the critic's law, but when he came to study Homer, he found that Nature and Homer were the same. Accordingly,

Addison's scholarship was almost exclusively Latin, though it was Vergilian rather than Horatian. Macaulay says of Addison's "Remarks on Italy"; "To the best of our remembrance, Addison does not mention Dante, Petrarch, Boccaccio, Bolardo, Berni, Lorenzo de' Medici, or Machiavelli. He coldly tells us that at Ferrara he saw the tomb of Ariosto, and that at Venice he heard the gondoliers sing verses of Tasso. But for Tasso and Ariosto he cared far less than for Valerius Flaccus and Sidonius Apollinaris. The gentle flow of the Ticino brings a line of Silius to his mind. The sulphurous stream of Albula suggests to him several passages of Martial. But he has not a word to say of the illustrious dead of Santa Croce; he crosses the wood of Ravenna without recollecting the specter huntsman, and wanders up and down Rimini without one thought of Francesca.

At Paris he had eagerly sought an introduction to Boileau; but he seems not to have been at all aware that at Florence he was in the vicinity of a poet with whom Boileau could not sustain a comparison: of the greatest lyric poet of modern times [!] Vincenzio Filicaja. . . The truth is that Addison knew little and cared less about the literature of modern Italy. His favorite models were Latin. His favorite critics were French. Half the Tuscan poetry that he had read seemed to him monstrous and the other half tawdry."

It is significant to note that there was no academy in England, but there was a critical tradition that was almost as influential. French critical gave the law: Boileau, Dacier, LeBossu, Rapin, Bouhours; English critics promulgated it: Dennis, Langbaine, Rymer, Gildon, and others now little read. Three writers of high authority in three successive generations—Dryden, Addison, and Johnson—consolidated a body of literary opinion which may be described, in the main, as classical, and as consenting, though with minor variations. Thus it was agreed on all hands that it was a writer's duty to be "correct."

It was well indeed to be "bold," but bold with discretion. Dryden thought Shakspeare a great poet than Jonson, but an inferior artist. He was to be admired, but not approved. Homer, again, it was generally conceded, was not so correct as Virgil, though he had more "fire." Chesterfield preferred Virgil to Homer, and both of them to Tasso. But of all epics the one he read with most pleasure was the "Henriade." As for "Paradise Lost," he could not read it through. William Walsh, "the muses' judge and friend," advised the youthful Pope that "there was one way still left open for him, by which he might excel any of his predecessors, which was by correctness; that though indeed we had several great poets, we as yet could boast of none that were perfectly correct; and that therefore he advised him to make this quality his particular study." "The best of the moderns in all language," he wrote to Pope, "are those that have the nearest copied the ancients."

In the drama, e.g., the observance of the unities was almost universally recommended, but by no means universally practiced. Johnson, himself a sturdy disciple of Dryden and Pope, exposed the fallacy of that stage illusion, on the supposed necessity of which the unities of time and place were defended. Yet Johnson, in his own tragedy

"Irene," conformed to the rules of Aristotle. He pronounced "Cato" "unquestionably the noblest production of Addison's genius," but acknowledge that its success had "introduced, or confirmed among us, the use of dialogue too declamatory, of unaffecting elegance and chill philosophy." On the other hand Addison had small regard for poetic justice, which Johnson thought ought to be observed. Addison praised old English ballads, which Johnson thought mean and foolish; and he guardedly commends "the fairy way of writing," a romantic foppery that Johnson despised.

Critical opinion was pronounced in favor of separating tragedy and comedy, and Addison wrote one sentence which condemns half the plays of Shakspeare and Fletcher: "The tragi-comedy, which is the product of the English theater, is one the most monstrous inventions that ever entered into a poet's thought." Dryden made some experiments in tragi-comedy, but, in general, classical comedy was pure comedy—the prose comedy of manners—and classical tragedy admitted no comic intermixture. Whether tragedy should be in rhyme, after the French manner, or in blank verse, after the precedent of the old English stage, was a moot point. Dryden at first argued for rhyme and used it in his "heroic plays"; and it is significant that he defended its use on the ground that it would act as a check upon the poet's fancy. But afterward he grew "weary of his much-loved mistress, rhyme," and went back to blank verse in his later plays.

As to poetry other than dramatic, the Restoration critics were at one in judging blank verse too "low" for a poem of heroic dimensions; and though Addison gave it the preference in epic poetry, Johnson was its persistent foe, and regarded it as little short of immoral. But for that matter, Gray could endure no blank verse outside of Milton. This is curious, that rhyme, a mediaeval invention, should have been associated in the last century with the classical school of poetry; while blank verse, the nearest English equivalent of the language of Attic tragedy, was a shibboleth of romanticizing poets, like Thomson and Akenside. The reason was twofold: rhyme came stamped with the authority of the French tragic alexandrine; and, secondly, it meant constraint where blank verse meant freedom, "ancient liberty, recovered to heroic poem from the troublesome and modern bondage of rhyming." Pope, among his many thousand rhymed couplets, has left no blank verse except the few lines contributed to Thomson's "Seasons." Even the heroic couplet as written by earlier poets was felt to have been too loose in structure. "The excellence and dignity of it," says Dryden, "were never fully known till Mr. Waller taught it; he first made writing easily an art; first showed us how to conclude the sense most commonly in distichs, which, in the verse of those before him, runs on for so many lines together, that the reader is out of breath to overtake it." All through the classical period the tradition is constant that Waller was the first modern English poet, the first correct versifier. Pope is praised by Johnson because he employed but sparingly the triplets and alexandrines by which Dryden sought to vary the monotony of the couplet; and he is censured by Cowper because, by force of his example, he "made poetry a mere mechanic art." Henceforth the distich was treated as a unit: the first line was balanced against the second, and frequently the first half of the line against the second half.

> "To err is human, to forgive divine."
>
> "And so obliging, that he ne'er obliged."
>
> "Charms strike the eye, but merit wins the soul," etc., etc.

This type of verse, which Pope brought to perfection, and to which he gave all the energy and variety of which it was capable, so prevailed in our poetry for a century or more that one almost loses sight of the fact that any other form was employed. The sonnet, for instance, disappeared entirely, until revived by Gray, Stillingfleet, Edwards, and Thomas Warton, about the middle of the eighteenth century. When the poets wished to be daring and irregular, they were apt to give vent in that species of pseudo-Pindaric ode which Cowley had introduced—a literary disease which, Dr. Johnson complained, infected the British muse with the notion that "he who could do nothing else could write like Pindar."

Sir Charles Eastlake in his "History of the Gothic Revival" testifies to this formal spirit from the point of view of another art than literature. "The age in which Batty Langley lived was an age in which it was customary to refer all matters of taste to rule and method. There was one standard of excellence in poetry—a standard that had its origin in the smooth distichs of heroic verse which Pope was the first to perfect, and which hundreds of later rhymers who lacked his nobler powers soon learned to imitate. In pictorial art, it was the grand school which exercised despotic sway over the efforts of genius and limited the painter's inventions to the field of Pagan mythology. In architecture, Vitruvius was the great authority. The graceful majesty of the Parthenon—the noble proportions of the temple of Theseus—the chaste enrichment which adorns the Choragic monument of Lysicrates, were ascribed less to the fertile imagination and refined perceptions of the ancient Greek, than to the dry and formal precepts which were invented centuries after their erection. Little was said of the magnificent sculpture which filled the metopes of the temple of the Minerva; but the exact height and breadth of the triglyphs between them were considered of the greatest importance. The exquisite drapery of caryatids and canephorae, no English artist, a hundred years ago, thought fit to imitate; but the cornices which they supposed were measured inch by inch with the utmost nicety. Ingenious devices were invented for enabling the artificer to reproduce, by a series of complicated curves, the profile of a Doric capital, which probably owed its form to the steady hand and uncontrolled taste of the designer. To put faith in many of the theories propounded by architectural authorities in the last century, would be to believe that some of the grandest monuments which the world has ever seen raised, owe their chief beauty to an accurate knowledge of arithmetic. The diameter of the column was divided into modules: the modules were divided into minutes; the minutes into fractions of themselves. A certain height was allotted to the shaft, another to the entablature. . . Sometimes the learned discussed how far apart the columns of a portico might be."

This kind of mensuration reminds one of the disputes between French critics as to whether the unity of time meant thirty hours, or twenty-four, or twelve, or the actual time that it took to act the play; or of the geometric method of the "Saturday papers" in the Spectator. Addison tries "Paradise Lost" by Aristotle's rules for the composition of an epic. Is it the narrative of a single great action? Does it begin in medias res, as is proper, or ab ovo Ledae, as Horace has said that an epic ought not? Does it bring in the introductory matter by way of episode, after the approved recipe of Homer and Vergil? Has it allegorical characters, contrary to the practice of the ancients? Does the poet intrude personally into his poem, thus mixing the lyric and epic styles? etc. Not a word as to Milton's puritanism, or his Weltanschauung, or the relation of his work to its environment. Nothing of that historical and sympathetic method—that endeavor to put the reader at the poet's point of view—by which modern critics, from Lessing to Sainte-Beuve, have revolutionized their art. Addison looks at "Paradise Lost" as something quite distinct from Milton: as a manufactured article to be tested by comparing it with standard fabrics by recognized makers, like the authors of the Iliad and Aeneid.

When the Queen Anne poetry took a serious turn, the generalizing spirit of the age led it almost always into the paths of ethical and didactic verse. "It stooped to truth and moralized its song," finding its favorite occupation in the sententious expression of platitudes—the epigram in satire, the maxim in serious work. It became a poetry of aphorisms, instruction us with Pope that

"Virtue alone is happiness below;"

or, with Young, that

"Procrastination is the thief of time;"

or, with Johnson, that

"Slow rises worth by poverty depressed."

When it attempted to deal concretely with the passions, it found itself impotent. Pope's "Epistle of Eloisa to Abelard" rings hollow: it is rhetoric, not poetry. The closing lines of "The Dunciad"—so strangely overpraised by Thackeray—with their metallic clank and grandiose verbiage, are not truly imaginative. The poet is simply working himself up to a climax of the false sublime, as an orator deliberately attaches a sounding peroration to his speech. Pope is always "heard," never "overheard."

The poverty of the classical period in lyrical verse is particularly significant, because the song is the most primitive and spontaneous kind of poetry, and the most direct utterance of personal feeling. Whatever else the poets of Pope's time could do, they could not sing. They are the despair of the anthologists. Here and there among the brilliant reasoners, raconteurs, and satirists in verse, occurs a clever epigrammatist like Prior, or a ballad writer like Henry Carey, whose "Sally in Our Alley" shows the singing, and not talking, voice, but hardly the lyric cry. Gay's "Blackeyed Susan" has genuine quality, though its rococo graces are more than half artificial. Sweet William is very much such an opera sailor-man as Bumkinet or Grubbinol is a shepherd, and his wooing is beribboned with conceits like these:

"If to fair India's coast we sail,
Thy eyes are seen in diamonds bright,
Thy breath is Afric's spicy gale,
Thy skin is ivory so white.

Thus every beauteous prospect that I view,
Wakes in my soul some charm of lovely Sue."

It was the same with the poetry of outward nature as with the poetry of human passion. In Addison's "Letter from Italy," in Pope's "Pastorals," and "Windsor Forest," the imagery, when not actually false, is vague and conventional, and the language abounds in classical insipidities, epithets that describe nothing, and generalities at second hand from older poets, who may once, perhaps, have written with their "eyes upon the object." Blushing Flora paints the enameled ground; cheerful murmurs fluctuate on the gale; Eridanus through flowery meadows strays; gay gilded scenes and shining prospects rise; while everywhere are balmy zephyrs, sylvan shades, winding vales, vocal shores, silver floods, crystal springs, feathered quires, and Phoebus and Philomel and Ceres' gifts assist the purple year. It was after this fashion that Pope rendered the famous moonlight passage in his translation of the Iliad:

"Then shine the vales, the rocks in prospect rise,
A flood of glory bursts from all the skies," etc.

"Strange to think of an enthusiast," says Wordsworth, "reciting these verses under the cope of a moonlight sky, without having his raptures in the least disturbed by a suspicion of their absurdity." The poetic diction against which Wordsworth protested was an outward sign of the classical preference for the general over the concrete. The vocabulary was Latinized because, in English, the mot propre is commonly a Saxon word, while its Latin synonym has a convenient indefiniteness that keeps the subject at arm's length. Of a similar tendency was the favorite rhetorical figure of personification, which gave a false air of life to abstractions by the easy process of spelling them with a capital letter. Thus:

"From bard to bard the frigid caution crept,
Till Declamation roared whilst Passion slept;

Yet still did Virtue deign the stage to tread,
Philosophy remained though Nature fled,. . .
Exulting Folly hailed the joyful day,
And Pantomime and Song confirmed her sway."

But circumstances or periphrasis was the capital means by which the Augustan poet avoided precision and attained nobility of style. It enabled him to speak of a woman as a "nymph," or a "fair"; of sheep as "the fleecy care"; of fishes as "the scaly tribe"; and of a picket fence as a "spiculated paling." Lowell says of Pope's followers: "As the master had made it an axiom to avoid what was mean or low, so the disciples endeavored to escape from what was common. This they contrived by the ready expedient of the periphrasis.

"For the direct appeal to Nature, and the naming of specific objects," says Gosse, "they substituted generalities and second-hand allusions. They no longer mentioned the gillyflower and the daffodil, but permitted themselves a general reference to Flora's vernal wreath. It was vulgar to say that the moon was rising; the gentlemanly expression was, 'Cynthia is lifting her silver horn!' Women became nymphs in this new phraseology, fruits became 'the treasures of Pomona,' a horse became 'the impatient courser.'

The result of coining these conventional counters for groups of ideas was that the personal, the exact, was lost in literature. Apples were the treasures of Pomona, but so were cherries, too, and if one wished to allude to peaches, they also were the treasures of Pomona. This decline from particular to general language was regarded as a great gain in elegance. It was supposed that to use one of these genteel counters, which passed for coin of poetic language, brought the speaker closer to the grace of Latinity. It was thought that the old direct manner of speaking was crude and futile; that a romantic poet who wished to allude to caterpillars could do so without any exercise of his ingenuity by simply introducing the word 'caterpillars,' whereas the classical poet had to prove that he was a scholar and a gentleman by inventing some circumlocution, such as 'the crawling scourge that smites the leafy plain.'. . . In the generation that succeeded Pope really clever writers spoke of a 'gelid cistern,' when they meant a cold bath, and 'the loud hunter-crew' when they meant a pack of foxhounds."

In fact it is wrong to suppose that the men of Pope's generation, including Pope himself, were altogether wanting in romantic feeling. There is a marked romantic accent in the Countess of Winchelsea's ode "To the Nightingale"; in her "Nocturnal Reverie"; in Parnell's "Night Piece on Death," and in the work of several Scotch poets, like Allan Ramsay and Hamilton of Bangour, whose ballad, "The Braces of Yarrow," is certainly a strange poem to come out of the heart of the eighteenth century. But these are eddies and back currents in the stream of literary tendency. Here it must be remembered that the literature of an age does not express its entire, but only its prevailing, spirit. There is commonly a latent, silent body of thought and feeling underneath which remains inarticulate, or nearly so.

4

Romanticism Amidst Spenserians

Apparently, Romanticism have assumed its present connotations around the mid-19th century, when the phenomenon to which it referred was already regarded as belonging to a completed past. Intellectual Romanticism pulled away form the philosophical rationalism and Neoclassicism of the Enlightenment, developing an alternative aesthetic of freedom from the 'dead' letter of formal rules and conventions.

First it is worth mentioning that dissatisfaction with a prevalent mood or fashion in literature is apt to express itself either in a fresh and independent criticism of life, or in a reversion to older types. But, as original creative genius is not always forthcoming, a literary revolution commonly begins with imitation. It seeks inspiration in the past, and substitutes a new set of models as different as possible from those which it finds currently followed. In every country of Europe the classical tradition had hidden whatever was most national, most individual, in its earlier culture, under a smooth, uniform veneer. To break away from modern convention, England and Germany, and afterward France, went back to ancient springs of national life; not always, at first, wisely, but in obedience to a true instinct.

How far did any knowledge or love of the old romantic literature of England survive among the contemporaries of

Dryden and Pope? It is not hard to furnish an answer to this question. The prefaces of Dryden, the critical treatises of Dennis, Winstanley, Oldmixon, Rymer, Langbaine, Gildon, Shaftesbury, and many others, together with hundreds of passages in prologues and epilogues to plays; in periodical essays like the Tatler and Spectator; in verse essays like Roscommon's, Mulgrave's and Pope's; in prefaces to various editions of Shakspeare and Spenser; in letters, memoirs, etc., supply a mass of testimony to the fact that neglect and contempt had, with a few exceptions, overtaken all English writers who wrote before the middle of the seventeenth century. The exceptions, of course, were those supreme masters whose genius prevailed against every change of taste: Shakspeare and Milton, and, in a less degree, Chaucer and Spenser. Of authors strictly mediaeval, Chaucer still had readers, and there were reprints of his works in 1687, 1721, and 1737, although no critical edition appeared until Tyrwhitt's in 1775-78.

It is probable, however, that the general reader, if he read Chaucer at all, read him in such modernized versions as Dryden's "Fables" and Pope's "January and May." Dryden's preface has some admirable criticism of Chaucer, although it is evident, from what he says about the old poet's versification, that the secret of Middle English scansion and pronunciation had already been lost. Prior and Pope, who seem to have been attracted chiefly to the looser among the "Canterbury Tales," made each a not very successful experiment at burlesque imitation of Chaucerian language. Outside of Chaucer, and except among antiquarians and professional scholars, there was no remembrance of the whole corpus poetarum of the English Middle Age: none of the metrical romances, rhymed chronicles, saints' legends, miracle plays, minstrel ballads, verse homilies, manuals of devotion, animal fables, courtly or popular allegories and love songs of the thirteenth, fourteenth, and fifteenth centuries.

Nor was there any knowledge or care about the

masterpieces of medieval literature in other languages than English; about such representative works as the "Nibelungenlied," the "Chanson de Roland," the "Roman de la Rose," the "Parzival" of Wolfram von Eschenbach, the "Tristan" of Gottfried of Strasburg, the "Arme Heinrich" of Harmann von Aue, the chronicles of Villehardouin, Joinville, and Froissart, the "Morte Artus," the "Dies Irae," the lyrics of the troubadour Bernart de Ventadour, and of the minnesinger Walter von der Vogelweide, the Spanish Romancero, the poems of the Elder Edda, the romances of "Amis et Amile" and "Aucassin et Nicolete," the writings of Villon, the "De Imitatione Christi" ascribed to Thomas à Kempis. Dante was a great name and fame, but he was virtually unread.

There is nothing strange about this; many of these things were still in manuscript and in unknown tongues, Old Norse, Old French, Middle High German, Middle English, Mediaeval Latin. It would be hazardous to assert that the general reader, or even the educated reader, of to-day has much more acquaintance with them at first hand than his ancestor of the eighteenth century; or much more acquaintance than he has with Aeschuylus, Thucydides, and Lucretius, at first hand. But it may be confidently asserted that he knows much more about them; that he thinks them worth knowing about; and that through modern, popular versions of them—through poems, historical romances, literary histories, essays and what not—he has in his mind's eye a picture of the Middle Age, perhaps as definite and fascinating as the picture of classical antiquity. That he has so is owing to the romantic movement. For the significant circumstance about the attitude of the last century toward the whole medieval period was, not its ignorance, but its incuriosity. It did not want to hear anything about it. Now and then, hints Pope, an antiquarian pedant, a university don, might affect an admiration for some obsolete author:

"Chaucer's worst ribaldry is learned by rote,
And beastly Skelton heads of houses quote:

One likes no language but the 'Faery Queen';
A Scot will fight for 'Christ's Kirk o' the Green.'"

But, furthermore, the great body of Elizabethan and Stuart literature was already obsolescent. Dramatists of the rank of Marlowe and Webster, poets like George Herbert and Robert Herrick—favorites with our own generation—prose authors like Sir Thomas Browne—from whom Coleridge and Emerson drew inspiration—had fallen into "the portion of weeds and outworn faces." Even writers of such recent, almost contemporary, repute as Donne, whom Carew had styled

"—a king who ruled, as he thought fit,
The universal monarch of wit":

Or as Cowley, whom Dryden called the darling of his youth, and who was esteemed in his own lifetime a better poet than Milton; even Donne and Cowley had no longer a following. Pope "versified" some of Donne's rugged satires, and Johnson quoted passages from him as examples of the bad taste of the metaphysical poets. This in the "Life of Cowley," with which Johnson began his "Lives of the Poets," as though Cowley was the first of the moderns.

The year of the Restoration (1660) draws a sharp line of demarcation between the old and the new. In 1675, the year after Milton's death, his nephew, Edward Philips, published "Theatrum Poetarum," a sort of biographical dictionary of ancient and modern authors. In the preface, he says: "As for the antiquated and fallen into obscurity from their former credit and reputation, they are, for the most part, those that have written beyond the verge of the present age; for let us look back as far as about thirty or forty years, and we shall find a profound silence of the poets beyond that time, except of some few dramatics."

This testimony is the more convincing, since Philips was something of a laudator temporis acti. He praises several old English poets and sneers at several new ones, such as Cleaveland and Davenant, who were high in favor with the royal party. He complains that nothing now "relishes so well as what is written in the smooth style of our present language, taken to be of late so much refined"; that "we should be so compliant with the French custom, as to follow set fashions"; that the imitation of Corneille has corrupted the English state; and that Dryden, "complying with the modified and gallantish humour of the time," has, in his heroic plays, "indulged a little too much to the French way of continual rime."

One passage, at least, in Philips' preface has been thought to be an echo of Milton's own judgment on the pretensions of the new school of poetry. "Wit, ingenuity, and learning in verse; even elegancy itself, though that comes nearest, are one thing. True native poetry is another; in which there is a certain air and spirit which perhaps the most learned and judicious in other arts do not perfectly apprehend, much less is it attainable by any study or industry. Nay, though all the laws of heroic poem, all the laws of tragedy were exactly observed, yet still this tour entrejeant—this poetic energy, if I may so call it, would be required to give life tò all the rest; which shines through the roughest, most unpolished, and antiquated language, and may haply be wanting in the most polite and reformed. Let us observe Spenser, with all his rusty, obsolete words, with all his rough-hewn clouterly verses; yet take him throughout, and we shall find in him a graceful and poetic majesty. In like manner, Shakspeare in spite of all his unfiled expressions, his rambling and indigested fancies—the laughter of the critical—yet must be confessed a poet above many that go beyond him to literature some degrees."

The laughter of the critical! Let us pause upon the phrase, for it is a key to the whole attitude of the Augustan mind toward "our old tragick poet." Shakspeare was already a national possession. Indeed it is only after the Restoration that we find any clear recognition of him, as one of the greatest—as perhaps himself the very greatest—of the dramatists of all time. For it is only after the Restoration that criticism begins. "Dryden," says Dr. Johnson, "may be properly considered as the father of English criticism, as the writer who first taught us to determine, upon principles, the merit of composition. . . Dryden's 'Essay of Dramatic Poesy' [1667] was the first regular and valuable treatise on the art of writing." The old theater was dead and Shakspeare now emerged from amid its ruins, as the one unquestioned legacy of the Elizabethan age to the world's literature. He was not only the favorite of the people, but in a critical time, and a time whole canons of dramatic art were opposed to his practice, he united the suffrages of all the authoritative leader of literacy opinion.

Pope's lines are conclusive as to the veneration in which Shakspeare's memory was held a century after his death.

"On Avon's banks, where flowers eternal blow,
If I but ask, if any weed can grow;
One tragic sentence if I dare deride
Which Betterton's grave action dignified . . .
How will our fathers rise up in a rage,
And swear, all shame is lost in George's age."

The Shakspearian tradition is unbroken in the history of English literature and of the English theater. His plays, in one form or another, have always kept the stage even in the most degenerate condition of public taste. Few handsomer tributes have been paid to Shakspeare's genius than were paid in prose and verse, by the critics of English classical age, from Dryden to Johnson. "To begin then with Shakspeare," says the former, in his "Essay of Dramatic Poesy," "he was the man who, of all modern and perhaps ancient poets, had the largest and most comprehensive soul." And, in the prologue to his adaptation of "The Tempest," he acknowledges that

"Shakspeare's magic could not copied be:
Within that circle none durst walk but he."

"The poet of whose works I have undertaken the revision," writes Dr. Johnson, "may now begin to assume the dignity of an ancient, and claim the privilege of established fame and prescriptive veneration."

"Each change of many-colored life he drew,
Exhausted worlds, and then imagined new."

Yet Dryden made many petulant, and Johnson many fatuous mistakes about Shakspeare; while such minor criticasters as Thomas Rymer and Mrs. Charlotte Lenox uttered inanities of blasphemy about the finest touches in "Macbeth" and "Othello." For if we look closer, we notice that everyone who bore witness to Shakspeare's greatness qualified his praise by an emphatic disapproval of his methods. He was a prodigious genius, but a most defective artist. He was the supremest of dramatic poets, but he did not know his business.

It did not apparently occur to anyone—except, in some degree, to Johnson—that there was an absurdity in this contradiction; and that the real fault was not in Shakspeare, but in the standards by which he was tried. Here are the tests which technical criticism has always been seeking to impose, and they are not confined to the classical period only. They are used by Sidney, who took the measure of the English buskin before Shakspeare had begun to write; by Jonson, who measured socks with him in his own day; by Matthew Arnold, who wanted an English Academy, but in whom the academic vaccine, after so long a transmission, worked but mildly.

Shakspeare violated the unities; his plays were neither right comedies nor right tragedies; he had small Latin and less Greek; he wanted art and sometimes sense, committing anachronisms and Bohemian shipwrecks; wrote hastily, did not blot enough, and failed of the grand style. He was "untaught, unpractised in a barbarous age"; a wild, irregular child of nature, ignorant of the rules, unacquainted with ancient models, succeeding—when he did succeed—by happy accident and the sheer force of genius; his plays were "roughdrawn," his plots lame, his speeches bombastic; he was guilty on every page of "some solecism or some notorious flaw in sense."

Langbaine, to be sure, defends him against Dryden's censure. But Dennis regrets his ignorance of poetic art and the disadvantages under which he lay from not being conversant with the ancients. If he had known his Sallust, he would have drawn a juster picture of Caesar; and if he had read Horace "Ad Pisones," he would have made a better Achilles. He complains that he makes the good and the bad perish promiscuously; and that in "Coriolanus"—a play which Dennis "improved" for the new stage—he represents Menenius as a buffoon and introduces the rabble in a most undignified fashion. Gildon, again, says that Shakspeare must have read Sidney's "Defence of Posey" and therefore, ought to have known the rules and that his neglect of them was owing to laziness. "Money seems to have been his aim more than reputation, and therefore he was always in a hurry . . . and he thought it time thrown away, to study regularity and order, when any confused stuff that came into his head would do his business and fill his house."

Pope voices the general sentiment of his school, as fairly as anyone, in the last words of his preface. "I will conclude by saying of Shakspeare that, with all his faults and with all the irregularity of his drama, one may look upon his works, in comparison of those that are more finished and regular, as upon an ancient, majestic piece of Gothic architecture compared with a neat, modern building. The latter is more elegant and glaring, but the former is more strong and solemn. . . It has much the greater variety, and much the nobler apartments, though we are often conducted to them by dark, odd and uncouth passages. Nor does the whole fail to strike us with greater reverence, though many of the parts are childish, ill-placed and unequal to its grandeur." This view of Shakspeare continued to be the rule until Coleridge and Schlegel taught the new century that this child of fancy was, in reality, a profound and subtle artist, but that the principles of his art—as is always the case with creative genius working freely and instinctively—were learned by practice, in the concrete, instead of being consciously thrown out by the workman himself into an abstract theoria; so that they have to be discovered by a reverent study of his work and lie deeper than the rules of French criticism. Schlegel, whose lectures on dramatic art were translated into English in 1815, speaks with indignation of the current English misunderstanding of Shakspeare. "That foreigners, and Frenchmen in particular, who frequently speak in the strangest language about antiquity and the Middle Age, as if cannibalism had been first put an end in Europe by Louis XIV., should entertain this opinion of Shakspeare might be pardonable. But that Englishmen should adopt such a calumniation . . . is to me incomprehensible."

In fact, the beginnings of the romantic movement in England were uncertain. There was a vague dissent from current literary estimates, a vague discontent with reigning literary modes, especially with the merely intellectual poetry then in vogue, which did not feed the soul. But there was, at first, no conscious, concerted effort toward something of creative activity. The new group of poets, partly contemporaries of Pope, partly successors to him—Thomson, Shenstone, Dyer, Akenside, Gray, Collins, and the Warton brothers—found their point of departure in the loving study and revival of old authors.

From what has been said of the survival of Shakspeare's influence it might be expected that his would have been the name paramount among the pioneers of English romanticism. There are several reasons why this was not the case. In the first place, the genius of the new poets was lyrical or descriptive, rather than dramatic. The divorce between literature and the stage had not yet, indeed, become total; and, in obedience to the expectation that every man of letters should try his hand at play-writing, Thomson, at least, as well as his friend and disciple Mallet, composed a number of dramas. But these were little better than failures even at the time; and while "The Seasons" has outlived all changes of taste, and "The Castle of Indolence" has never wanted admirers, tragedies like "Agamemnon" and "Sophonisba" have been long forgotten.

An imitation of Shakspeare to any effective purpose must obviously have take the shape of a play; and neither Gray nor Collins nor Akenside, nor any of the group, was capable of a play. Inspiration of a kind, these early romanticists did draw from Shakspeare. Verbal reminiscences of him abound in Gray. Collins was a diligent student of his works.

His "Dirge in Cymbeline" is an exquisite variation on a Shakspearian theme. In the delirium of his last sickness, he told Warton that he had found in an Italian novel the long-sought original of the plot of "The Tempest." It is noteworthy, by the way, that the romanticists were attracted to the poetic, as distinguished from the dramatic, aspect of Shakspeare's genius; to those of his plays in which fairy lore and supernatural machinery occur, such as "The Tempest" and "A Midsummer Night's Dream."

Again, the stage has a history of its own, and, in so far as it was now making progress of any kind, it was not in the direction of a more poetic or romantic drama, but rather toward prose tragedy and the sentimental comedy of domestic life, what the French call la tragédie bourgeoise and la comédie larmoyante.

In truth the theater was now dying; and though, in the comedies of Goldsmith and Sheridan, it sent up one bright, expiring gleam, the really dramatic talent of the century had already sought other channels in the novels of Richardson, Fielding, and Smollett.

After all, a good enough reason why the romantic movement did not begin with imitation of Shakspeare is the fact that Shakspeare is inimitable. He has no one manner that can be caught, but a hundred manners; is not the poet of romance, but of humanity; nor medieval, but perpetually modern and contemporaneous in his universality. The very familiarity of his plays, and their continuous performance, although in mangled forms, was a reason why they could take little part in a literary revival; for what has never been forgotten cannot be revived. To Germany and France, at a later date, Shakspeare came with the shock of a discovery and begot Schiller and Victor Hugo. In the England of the eighteenth century he begot only Ireland's forgeries.

If there is any poet who is par excellence the poet of romance, whose art is the antithesis of Pope's, it is the poet of the "Faërie Queene." To ears that had heard from childhood the tinkle of the couplet, with its monotonously recurring rhyme, its inevitable caesura, its narrow imprisonment of the sense, it must have been a relief to turn to the amplitude of Spencer's stanza, "the full strong sail of his great verse." To a generation surfeited with Pope's rhetorical devices—antithesis, climax, anticlimax—and fatigued with the unrelaxing brilliancy and compression of his language; the escape from epigrams and point (snap after snap, like a pack of fire-crackers), from a style which has made his every other line a proverb or current quotation—the escape from all this into Spenser's serene, leisurely manner, copious Homeric similes, and lingering detail must have seemed most restful. To go from Pope to Spenser was to exchange platitudes, packed away with great verbal cunning in neat formulas readily portable by the memory, for a wealth of concrete images: to exchange saws like,

"A little learning is a dangerous thing,"

for a succession of richly colored pictures by the greatest painter among English poets. It was to exchange the most prosaic of our poets—a poet about whom question has arisen whether he is a poet at all—for the most purely poetic of our poets, "the poet's poet." And finally, it was to exchange the world of everyday manners and artificial society for an imaginary kingdom of enchantment, "out of space, out of time."

English poetry has oscillated between the poles of Spenser and Pope. The poets who have been accepted by the race as most truly national, poets like Shakspeare, Milton, and Byron, have stood midway. Neither Spenser nor Pope satisfies long. We weary, in time, of the absence of passion and intensity in Spenser, his lack of dramatic power, the want of actuality in his picture of life, the want of brief energy and nerve in his style; just as we weary of Pope's inadequate sense of beauty. But at a time when English poetry had abandoned its true function—the refreshment and elevation of the soul through the imagination—Spenser's poetry, the poetry of ideal beauty, formed the most natural corrective. Whatever its deficiencies, it was not, at any rate, "conceived and composed in his wits."

It is pertinent to note that Spenser had not fared so well as Shakspeare under the change which came over public taste after the Restoration. The age of Elizabeth had no literary reviews or book notices, and its critical remains are of the scantiest. But the complimentary verses by many hands published with the "Faërie Queene" and the numerous references to Spenser in the whole poetic literature of the time, leave no doubt as to the fact that his contemporaries accorded him the foremost place among English poets.

The tradition of his supremacy lasted certainly to the middle of the seventeenth century, if not beyond. His influence is visible not only in the work of professed disciples like Giles and Phineas Fletcher, the pastoral poet William

Browne, and Henry More, the Cambridge Platonist, but in the verse of Jonson, Fletcher, Milton, and many others. Milton confessed to Dryden that Spenser was his "poetical father." Dryden himself and Cowley, whose practice is so remote from Spenser's, acknowledged their debt to him. The passage from Cowley's essay "On Myself" is familiar: "I remember when I began to read, and to take some pleasure in it, there was wont to lie in my mother's parlour (I know not by what accident, for she herself never read any book but of devotion—but there was wont to lie) Spenser's works. This I happened to fall upon, and was infinitely delighted with the stories of the knights and giants and monsters and brave houses which I found everywhere there (thought my understanding had little to do with all this), and, by degrees, with the tinkling of the rime and dance of the numbers; so that I think I had read him all over before I was twelve years old, and was thus made a poet as irremediably as a child is made an eunuch." It is a commonplace that Spenser has made more poets than any other one writer. Even Pope, whose empire he came back from Fairyland to overthrow, assured Spence that he had read the "Faërie Queene" with delight when he was a boy, and re-read it with equal pleasure in his last years. Indeed, it is too readily assumed that writers are insensible to the beauties of an opposite school. Pope was quite incapable of appreciating it. He took a great liking to Allan Ramsay's "Gentle Shepherd"; he admired "The Seasons," and did Thomson the honor to insert a few lines of his own in "Summer." Among his youthful parodies of old English poets is one piece entitled "The Alley," a not over clever burlesque of the famous description of the Bower of Bliss.

As for Dryden, his reverence for Spenser is qualified by the same sort of critical disapprobation which we noticed in his eulogies of Shakspeare. He says that the "Faërie Queene" has no uniformity: the language is not so obsolete as is commonly supposed, and is intelligible after some practice; but the choice of stanza is unfortunate, though in spite of it, Spenser's verse is more melodious than any other English poet's except Mr. Waller's. Ambrose Philips—Namby Pamby Philips—whom Thackeray calls "a dreary idyllic cockney," appealed to "The Shepherd's Calendar" as his model, in the introduction to his insipid "Pastorals," 1709. Steele, in No. 540 of the Spectator (November 19, 1712), printed some mildly commendatory remarks about Spenser. Altogether it is clear that Spenser's greatness was accepted, rather upon trust, throughout the classical period, but that this belief was coupled with a general indifference to his writings. Addison's lines in his "Epistle to Sacheverel; an Account of the Greatest English Poets," 1694, probably represent accurately enough the opinion of the majority of readers:

"Old Spenser next, warmed with poetic rage,
In ancient tales amused a barbarous age;
An age that, yet uncultivated and rude,
Wher'er the poet's fancy led, pursued,
Through pathless fields and unfrequented floods,
To dens of dragons and enchanted woods.
But now the mystic tale, that pleased of yore,
Can charm an understanding age no more.
The long-spun allegories fulsome grow,
While the dull moral lies too plain below,
We view well pleased at distance all the sights
Of arms and palfreys, battles, fields and fights,
And damsels in distress and courteous knights,
But when we look too near, the shades decay
And all the pleasing landscape fades away."

Addison acknowledged to Spencer that, when he wrote this passage, he had never read Spenser! As late as 1754 Thomas Warton speaks of him as "this admired but neglected poet," and Kitchin asserts that "between 1650 and 1750 there are but few notices of him, and a very few editions of his works." There was a reprint of Spenser's works—being the third folio of the "Faërie Queene"—in 1679, but no critical edition till 1715. Meanwhile the title of a book issued in 1687 shows that Spenser did not escape that process of "improvement" which we have seen applied to Shakspeare: "Spenser Redivivus; containing the First Book of the 'Faëry Queene.' His Essential Design Preserved, but his Obsolete Language and Manner of Verse totally laid aside. Delivered in Heroic Numbers by a Person of Quality." The preface praises Spenser, but declares that "his style seems no less unintelligible at this day than the obsoletest of our English or Saxon dialect." One instance of this deliverance into heroic numbers must suffice:

"By this the northern wagoner had set
His sevenfold team behind the steadfast star
That was in ocean waves yet never wet,
But firm is fixed, and sendeth light from far
To all that in the wide deep wandering are."

—*Spenser.*

Remarkably, John Hughes published in 1715 his edition of Spenser's works in six volumes. This was the first attempt at a critical text of the poet, and was accompanied with a biography, a glossary, an essay on allegorical poetry, and some remarks on the "Faërie Queene." It is curious to find in the engravings, from designs by Du Guernier, which illustrate Hughes' volumes, that Spenser's knights wore the helmets and body armor of the Roman legionaries, over which is occasionally thrown something that looks very much like a toga. The lists in which they run a tilt have the façade of a Greek temple for a background. The house of Busyrane is Louis Quatorze architecture, and Amoret is chained to a renaissance column with Corinthian capital and classical draperies. Hughes' glossary of obsolete terms includes words which are in daily use by modern writers: aghast, baleful, behest, bootless, carol, craven, dreary, forlorn, foray, guerdon, plight, welkin, yore. If words like these, and like many which Warton annotates in his "Observations," really needed explanation, it is a striking proof, not only of the degree in which our older poets had been forgotten, but also of the poverty to which the vocabulary of English poetry had been reduced by 1700.

Remarkably, in his prefatory remarks to the "Faërie Queene," the editor expresses the customary regrets that the poet should have chosen so defective a stanza, "so romantick a story," and a model, or framework for the whole, which appears so monstrous when "examined by the rules of epick poetry"; makes the hackneyed comparison between Spenser's work and Gothic architecture, and apologizes for his author, on the ground that, at the time when he wrote, "the remains of the old Gothick chivalry were not quite abolished." "He did not much revive the curiosity of the public," says Johnson, in his life of Hughes; "for near thirty years elapsed before his edition was reprinted." Editions of the "Faërie Queene" came thick and fast about the middle of the century. One (by Birch) was issued in 1751, and three in 1758; including the important edition by Upton, who, of all Spenser's commentators, has entered most elaborately into the interpretation of the allegory.

In fact, the interval had appeared, in gradually increasing numbers, that series of Spenserian imitations which forms an interesting department of eighteenth-century verse. The series was begun by a most unlikely person, Matthew Prior, whose "Ode to the Queen," 1706, was in a ten-lined modification of Spenser's stanza and employed a few archaisms like weet and ween, but was very unspenserian in manner. As early as the second decade of the century, the horns of Elfland may be heard faintly blowing in the poems of the Rev. Samuel Croxall, the translator of Aesop's "Fables." Mr. Gosse quotes Croxall's own description of his poetry, as designed "to set off the dry and insipid stuff" of the age with "a whole piece of rich and glowing scarlet."

His two pieces "The Vision," 1715, and "The Fair Circassian," 1720, though written in the couplet, exhibit a rosiness of color and a luxuriance of imagery manifestly learned from Spenser. In 1713 he had published under the pseudonym of Nestor Ironside, "An Original Canto of Spenser," and in 1714 "Another Original Canto," both, of course, in the stanza of the "Faërie Queene." The example thus set was followed before the end of the century by scores of poets, including many well-known names, like Akenside, Thomson, Shenstone, and Thomas Warton, as well as many second-rate and third-rate versifiers.

It is noteworthy that many, if not most, of the imitations were at first undertaken in a spirit of burlesque; as is plain not only from the poems themselves, but from the correspondence of Shenstone and others. The antiquated speech of an old author is in itself a challenge to the parodist: teste our modern ballad imitations. There is something ludicrous about the very look of antique spelling, and in the sound of words like eftsoones and perdy; while the sign Ye Olde Booke Store, in Old English text over a bookseller's door, strikes the public invariably as a most merry conceited jest; especially if the first letter be pronounced as a y, instead of, what it really is, a mere abbreviation of th. But in order that this may be so, the language travestied should not be too old. There would be nothing amusing, for example, in a burlesque imitation of Beowulf, because the Anglo-Saxon of the original is utterly strange to the modern reader.

It is conceivable that quick-witted Athenians of the time of Aristophanes might find something quaint in Homer's Ionic dialect, akin to that quaintness which we find in Chaucer; but a Grecian of to-day would need to be very Attic indeed, to detect any provocation to mirth in the use of the genitive in-oio, in place of the genitive in-ou. Again, as one becomes familiar with an old author, he ceases to be conscious of his archaism: the final e in Chaucer no longer strikes him as funny, nor even the circumstance that he speaks of little birds as smalë fowlës. And so it happened, that poets in the eighteenth century who began with burlesque imitation of the "Faërie Queen" soon fell in love with its serious beauties.

Remarkably, the only poems in this series that have gained permanent footing in the literature are Shenstone's "Schoolmistress" and Thomson's "Cast of Indolence." But a brief review of several other members of the group will be advisable. Two of them were written at Oxford in honor of the marriage of Frederick, Prince of Wales in 1736: one by Richard Owen Cambridge; the other by William Thompson, then bachelor of arts and afterward fellow of Queen's College. Prince Fred, it will be remembered, was a somewhat flamboyant figure in the literary and personal gossip of his day. He quarreled with his father, George II, who "hated boetry and bainting," and who was ironically fed with soft dedication by Pope in his "Epistle to Augustus"; also with his father's prime minister, Sir Robert Walpole, "Bob, the poet's foe."

He left the court in dudgeon and set up an opposition court of his own where he rallied about him men of letters, who had fallen into a neglect that contrasted strangely with their former importance in the reign of Queen Anne. Frederick's chief ally in this policy was his secretary, George Lord Lyttelton, the elegant if somewhat amateurish author of "Dialogues of the Dead" and other works; the friend of Fielding, the neighbor of Shenstone at Hagley, and the patron of Thomson, for whom he obtained the sinecure post of Surveyor of the Leeward Islands.

It is pertinent to note that Cambridge's spousal verses were in a ten-lined stanza. His "Archimage," written in the strict Spenserian stanza, illustrates the frequent employment of this form in occasional pieces of a humorous intention. It describes a domestic boating party on the Thames, one of the oarsmen being a family servant and barber-surgeon, who used to dress the chaplain's hair.

Remarkably, Thompson's experiments, on the contrary, were quite serious. He had genuine poetic feeling, but little talent. In trying to reproduce Spenser's richness of imagery and the soft modulation of his verse, he succeeds only in becoming tediously ornate. His stanzas are nerveless, though not unmusical. His college exercise, "The Nativity," 1736, is a Christmas vision which comes to the shepherd boy Thomalin, as he is piping on the banks of Isis.

It employs the pastoral machinery, includes a masque of virtues,—Faith, Hope, Mercy, etc.,—and closes with a compliment to Pope's "Messiah." The preface to his "Hymn to May," has some bearing upon our inquiries: "As Spenser is the most descriptive and florid of all our English writers, I attempted to imitate his manner in the following vernal poem. I have been very sparing of the antiquated words which are too frequent in most of the imitations of this author. . . His lines are most musically sweet, and his descriptions most delicately abundant, even to a wantonness of painting, but still it is the music and painting of nature. We find no ambitious ornaments or epigrammatical turns in his writings, but a beautiful simplicity which pleases far above the glitter of pointed wit." The "Hymn to May" is in the seven-lined stanza of Phineas Fletcher's "Purple Island"; a poem, says Thompson, "scarce heard of in this age, yet the best in the allegorical way in the English language."

William Wilkie, a Scotch minister and professor, of eccentric habits and untidy appearance, published, in 1759, "A Dream: in the Manner of Spenser," which may be mentioned here not for its own sake, but for the evidence that it affords of a growing impatience of classical restraints. The piece was a pendant to Wilkie's epic, the "Epigoniad." Walking by the Tweed, the poet falls asleep and has a vision of Homer, who reproaches him with the bareness of style in his "Epigoniad." The dreamer puts the blame upon the critics,

Further, one of the earlier Spenserians was Gilbert

West, the translator of Pindar, who published, in 1739, *"On the Abuse of Travelling: A Canto in Imitation of Spenser."* Another imitation, "Education," appeared in 1751. West was a very tame poet, and the only quality of Spenser's which he succeeded in catching was his prolixity. He used the allegorical machinery of the "Faërie Queene" for moral and mildly satirical ends. Thus, in "The Abuse of Traveling," the Red Cross Knight is induced by Archimago to embark in a painted boat steered by Curiosity, which wafts him over to a foreign shore where he is entertained by a bevy of light damsels whose leader "hight Politessa," and whose blandishments the knight resists. Thence he is conducted to a stately castle (the court of Louis XV. whose minister—perhaps Cardinal Fleury?—is "an old and rankled mage"); and finally to Rome, where a lady yclept Vertù holds court in the ruins of the Colosseum, among mimes, fiddlers, pipers, eunuchs, painters, and ciceroni.

The canto on "Education" narrates how a fairy knight, while conducting his young son to the house of Paidia, encounters the giant Custom and worsts him in single combat. There is some humor in the description of the stream of science into which the crowd of infant learners are unwillingly plunged, and upon whose margin stands

"A birchen *grove that, waving from the shore,*
Aye cast upon the tide its falling bud
And with its bitter juice empoisoned all the flood."

Remarkably, the piece is a tedious arraignment of the pedantic methods of instruction in English schools and colleges. A passage satirizing the artificial style of gardening will be cited later. West had a country-house at Wickham, in Kent, where, says Johnson, "he was very often visited by Lyttelton and Pitt; who, when they were weary of faction and debates, used at Wickham to find books and quiet, a decent table and literary conversation. There is at Wickham, a walk made by Pitt." Like many contemporary poets, West interested himself in landscape gardening, and some of his shorter pieces belong to that literature of inscriptions to which Lyttelton, Akenside, Shenstone, Mason, and others contributed so profusely. It may be said for his Spenserian imitations that their archaisms are unusually correct—if that be any praise—a feature which perhaps recommended them to Gray, whose scholarship in this, as in all points, was nicely accurate.

The obligation to be properly "obsolete" in vocabulary was one that rested heavily on the consciences of most of these Spenserian imitators. "The Squire of Dames," for instance, by the wealthy Jew, Moses Mendez, fairly bristles with seld-seen costly words, like benty, frannion, etc., which it would have puzzled Spenser himself to explain.

One of the pleasantest outcomes of this literary fashion was William Shenstone's "Schoolmistress," published in an unfinished shape in 1737 and, as finally completed, in 1742. This is an affectionate half-humorous description of the little dame-school of Shenstone's—and of everybody's—native village, and has the true idyllic touch. Goldsmith evidently had it in memory when he drew the picture of the school in his "Deserted Village."

The application to so humble a theme of Spenser's stately verse and grave, ancient words gives a very quaint effect. The humor of "The Schoolmistress" is genuine, not dependent on the more burlesque, as in Pope's and Cambridge's experiments; and it is warmed with a certain tenderness, as in the incident of the hen with her brood of chickens, entering the open door of the schoolhouse in search of crumbs, and of the grief of the little sister who witnesses her brother's flogging, and of the tremors of the urchins who have been playing in the dame's absence.

Remarkably, the only one among the professed scholars of Spenser who caught the glow and splendor of the master was James Thomson. It is the privilege of genius to be original even in its imitations. Thomson took shape and hue from Spenser, but added something of his own, and the result has a value quite independent of its success as a reproduction. "The Castle of Indolence," 1748, is a fine poem; at least the first part of it is, for the second book is tiresomely allegorical, and somewhat involved in plot. There is a magic art in the description of the "land of drowsy-head," with its "listless climate" always "atween June and May," its "stockdove's plaint amid the forest deep," its hillside woods of solemn pines, its gay castles in the summer clouds, and its murmur of the distance main. The nucleus of Thomson's conception is to be found in Spenser's House of Morpheus ("Faërie Queene," book i. canto i. 41), and his Country of Idlesse is itself an anticipation of Tennyson's *Lotus Land,* but verse like this was something new in the poetry of the eighteenth century:

> "Was nought around but images of rest:
> Sleep-soothing groves and quiet lawns between;
> And flowery beds that slumberous influence kest,
> From poppies breathed; and beds of pleasant green,
> Where never yet was creeping creatures seen.
> "Meantime unnumbered glittering streamlets played
> And hurlëd everywhere their waters sheen;
> That, as they bickered through the sunny glade,
> Though restless still themselves, a lulling murmur made."

"The Castle of Indolence" had the romantic iridescence, the "atmosphere" which is lacking to the sharp contours of Augustan verse. That is to say, it produces an effect which cannot be wholly accounted for by what the poet says; an effect which is wrought by subtle sensations awakened by the sound and indefinite associations evoked by the words. The secret of this art the poet himself cannot communicate. But poetry of this kind cannot be translated into prose—as Pope's can—any more than music can be translated into speech, without losing its essential character. Like Spenser, Thomson was an exquisite colorist and his art was largely pictorial. But he has touches of an imagination which is rarer, if not higher in kind, than anything in Spenser. The fairyland of Spenser is an unreal, but hardly an unearthly region. He seldom startles by glimpses behind the curtain which hangs between nature and the supernatural, as in Milton's

"Airy tongues that syllable men's names
On sands and shores and desert wildernesses."

There is something of this power in one stanza, at least, of "The Castle of Indolence:"

"As when a shepherd of the Hebrid Isles,
Placed far amid the melancholy main
(Whether it be lone fancy him beguiles,
Or that aerial beings sometimes deign
To stand embodied to our sense plain),
The whilst in ocean Phoebus dips his wain,
A vast assembly moving to and fro,
Then all at once in air dissolves the wondrous show."

It may be guessed that Johnson and Boswell, in their tour to the Hebrides or Western Islands, saw nothing of the "spectral puppet play" hinted at in this passage—the most imaginative in any of Spenser's school till we get to Keats'

"Magic casements opening on the foam
Of perilous seas in fairy lands forlorn."

William Julius Mickle, the translator of the "Lusiad," was a more considerable poet than any of the Spenserian imitators thus far reviewed, with the exception of Thomson and the possible exception of Shenstone. He wrote at least two poems that are likely to be remembered. One of these was the ballad of "Cumnor Hall" which suggested Scott's "Kenilworth," and came near giving its name to the novel. The other was the dialect song of "The Mariner's Wife," which Burns admired so greatly:

"Sae true his heart, sae smooth his speech,
His breath like caller air,
His very foot has music in't,
As he comes up the stair,
For there's nae luck about the house,
There is nae luck at a',
There's little pleasure in the house
When our gudeman's awa',"

Mickle, like Thomson, was a Scotchman who came to London to push his literary fortunes. He received some encouragement from Lyttelton, but was disappointed in his hopes of any substantial aid from the British Maecenas. His biographer informs us that "about his thirteenth year, on Spenser's 'Faërie Queene' falling accidentally in his way, he was immediately struck with the picturesque descriptions of that much admired ancient bard and powerfully incited to imitate his style and manner." In 1767 Mickle published "The Concubine," a Spenserian poem in two cantos. In the preface to his second edition, 1778, in which the title was changed to "Syr Martyn," he said that: "The fullness and wantonness of description, the quaint simplicity, and, above all, the ludicrous, of which the antique phraseology and manner of Spenser are so happily and peculiarly susceptible, inclined him to esteem it not solely as the best, but the only mode of composition adapted to his subject."

"Syr Martyn" is a narrative poem not devoid of animation, especially where the author forgets his Spenser. But in the second canto he feels compelled to introduce an absurd allegory, in which the nymph Dissipation and her henchman Self-Imposition conduct the hero to the cave of Discontent.

A reader would be guilty of no very bad guess who should assign this stanza—which Scott greatly admired—to one of he Spenserian passages that prelude the "Lady of the Lake."

But it is needless to extend this catalogue any farther. By the middle of the century Spenserian had become so much the fashion as to provoke a rebuke from Dr. Johnson, who prowled up and down before the temple of the British Muses like a sort of classical watch-dog. "The imitation of Spenser," said the Rambler of May 14, 1751, "by the influence of some men of learning and genius, seems likely to gain upon the age. . . To imitate the fictions and sentiments of Spenser can incur no reproach, for allegory is perhaps one of the most pleasing vehicles of instruction.

But I am very far from extending the same respect to his diction or his stanza. His style was, in his own words and peculiarities of phrase, and so remote from common use that Jonson boldly pronounces him to have written no language. His stanza is at once difficult and unpleasing: tiresome to the ear by its uniformity, and to the attention by its length. . . Life is surely given us for other purposes than to gather what our ancestors have wisely thrown away and to learn what is of no value but because it has been forgotten." In his "Life of West," Johnson says of West's imitations of Spenser, "Such compositions are not to be reckoned among the great achievements of intellect, because their effect is local and temporary: they appeal not to reason or passion, but to memory, and presuppose an accidental or artificial state of mind. An imitation of Spenser is nothing to a reader, however acute, by whom Spenser has never been perused."

The nice points of a parody are lost upon a reader unacquainted with the thing parodied. And as for serious imitations, the more cleverly a copyist follows his copy, the less value his work will have. The eighteenth-century Spenserians, like West, Cambridge, and Lloyd, who stuck most closely to their pattern, oblivion has covered. Their real service was done in reviving a taste for a better kind of poetry than the kind in vogue, and particularly in restoring to English verse a stanza form, which became so noble an instrument in the hands of later poets, who used it with as much freedom and vigor as if they had never seen the "Faërie Queene." One is seldom reminded of Spenser while reading "Childe Harold" or "Adonais" or "The Eve of Saint Agnes"; but in reading West or Cambridge, or even in reading Shenstone and Thomson, one is reminded of him at every turn. Yet if it was necessary to imitate anyone, it might be answered to Dr. Johnson that it was better to imitate Spenser than Pope. In the imitation of Spenser lay, at least, a future, a development; while the imitation of Pope was conducting steadily toward Darwin's "Botanic Garden."

It remains to notice one more document in the history of this Spenserian revival, Thomas Warton's "Observations on the Faërie Queen," 1754. Warton wrote with a genuine delight in his subject. His tastes were frankly romantic. But the apologetic air which antiquarian scholars assumed, when venturing to recommend their favorite studies to the attention of a classically minded public, is not absent from Warton's commentary. He writes as if he felt the pressure of an unsympathetic atmosphere all about him. "We who live in the days of writing by rule are apt to try every composition by those laws which we have been taught to think the sole criterion of excellence.

Critical taste is universally diffused, and we require the same order and design which every modern performance is expected to have, in poems where they never were regarded or intended. . . If there be any poem whose graces please because they are situated beyond the reach of art . . . it is this. In reading Spenser, if the critic is not satisfied, yet the reader is transported." "In analyzing the plan and conduct of this poem, I have so far tried it by epic rules, as to demonstrate the inconveniences and incongruities which the poet might have avoided, had he been more studious of design and uniformity. It is true that his romantic materials claim great liberties; but no materials exclude order and perspicacity." Warton assures the reader that Spenser's language is not "so difficult and obsolete as it is generally supposed to be;" and defends him against Hume's censure, that "Homer copied true natural manners . . . but the pencil of the English poet was employed in drawing the affectations and conceits and fopperies of chivalry."

Yet he began his commentary with the stock denunciations of "Gothic ignorance and barbarity." "At the renaissance it might have been expected that, instead of the romantic manner of poetical composition . . . a new and more legitimate taste of writing would have succeeded. . . But it was a long time before such a change was effected. We find Ariosto, many years after the revival of letters, rejecting truth for magic, and preferring the ridiculous and incoherent excursions of Boiardo to the propriety and uniformity of the Grecian and Roman models. Nor did the restoration of ancient learning produce any effectual or immediate improvement in the state of criticism. Beni, one of the most celebrated critics of the sixteenth century, was still so infatuated with a fondness for the old Provençal vein, that he ventured to write a regular dissertation, in which he compares Ariosto with Homer." Warton says again, of Ariosto and the Italian renaissance poets whom Spenser followed, "I have found no fault in general with their use of magical machinery; notwithstanding I have so far conformed to the reigning maxims of modern criticism as to recommend classical propriety."

Notwithstanding this prudent determination to conform, the author takes heart in his second volume to speak out as follows about the pseudo-classic poetry of his own age: "A poetry succeeded in which imagination gave way to correctness, sublimity of description to delicacy of sentiment, and majestic imagery to conceit and epigram. Poets began now to be more attentive to words than to things and objects. The nicer beauties of happy expression were preferred to the daring strokes of great conception. Satire, that bane of the sublime, was imported from France. The muses were debauched at court; and polite life and familiar manners became their only themes."

It is pertinent to note that the time these words were written Spenser had done his work. Color, music, fragrance were stealing back again into English song, and "golden-tongued romance with serene lute" stood at the door of the new age, waiting for it to open.

5

Thomas Warton and His School

First it is pertinent to note that though Romantic the literary movement had already begun to take a retrospective turn, few distinctly mediaeval elements were yet in evidence. Neither the literature of the monk nor the literature of the knight had suffered resurrection. It was not until about 1760 that writers began to gravitate decidedly toward the Middle Ages.

The first peculiarly mediaeval type that contrived to secure a foothold in eighteenth-century literature was the hermit, a figure which seems to have had a natural attraction, not only for romanticizing poets like Shenstone and Collins, but for the whole generation of verse writers from Parnell to Goldsmith, Percy and Beattie—each of whom composed a "Hermit"—and even for the authors of "Rasselas" and "Tom Jones," in whose fictions he becomes a stock character, as a fountain of wisdom and of moral precepts.

It can safely be surmised that the true pioneers of the mediaeval revival were the Warton brothers. "The school of Warton" was a term employed, not without disparaging implications, by critics who had no liking for antique minstrelsy. Joseph and Thomas Warton were the sons of Thomas Warton, vicar of Basingstoke, who had been a fellow of Magdalen and Professor of Poetry at Oxford; which latter position was afterward filled by the younger of his two sons. It is interesting to note that a volume of verse by Thomas Warton, Sr., posthumously printed in

1748, includes a Spenserian imitation and translations of two passages from the "Song of Ragner Lodbrog," an eleventh-century Viking, after the Latin version quoted by Sir Wm. Temple in his essay "Of Heroic Virtue"; so that the romantic leanings of the Warton brothers seem to be an instance of heredity.

Joseph was educated at Winchester,—where Collins was his schoolfellow—and both of the brothers at Oxford. Joseph afterward became headmaster of Winchester, and lived till 1800, surviving his younger brother ten years. Thomas was always identified with Oxford, where he resided for forty-seven years. He was appointed, in 1785, Camden Professor of History in the university, but gave no lectures. In the same year he was chosen to succeed Whitehead, as Poet Laureate. Both brothers were men of a genial, social temper. Joseph was a man of some elegance; he was fond of the company of young ladies, went into general society, and had a certain renown as a drawing-room wit and diner-out. He used to spend his Christmas vacations in London, where he was a member of Johnson's literary club. Thomas, on the contrary, who waxed fat and indolent in college cloisters, until Johnson compared him to a turkey cock, was careless in his personal habits and averse to polite society. He was the life of a common room at Oxford, romped with the schoolboys when he visited Dr. Warton at Winchester, and was said to have a hankering after pipes and ale and the broad mirth of the taproom.

Both Wartons had an odd passion for military parades; and Thomas—who was a believer in ghosts—used secretly to attend hangings. They were also remarkably harmonious in their tastes and intellectual pursuits, eager students of old English poetry, Gothic architecture, and British antiquities. So far as enthusiasm, fine critical taste, and elegant scholarship can make men poets, the Wartons were poets. But their work was quite unoriginal. Many of their poems can be taken to pieces and assigned, almost line by line and phrase by phrase, to Milton, Thomson, Spenser,

Shakspeare, Gray. They had all of our romantic poet Longfellow's dangerous gifts of sympathy and receptivity, without a tenth part of his technical skill, or any of his real originality as an artist.

No exaggeration, it can safely be surmised that a literary movement which reverts to the past for its inspiration is necessarily also a learned movement. Antiquarian scholarship must lead the way. The picture of an extinct society has to be pieced together from the fragments at hand, and this involves special research. So long as this special knowledge remains the exclusive possession of professional antiquaries like Gough, Hearne, Bentham, Perry, Grose, it bears no fruit in creative literature. It produces only local histories, surveys of cathedrals and of sepulchral monuments, books about Druidic remains, Roman walls and coins, etc., etc.

It was only when men of imagination and of elegant tastes were enlisted in such pursuits that the dry stick of antiquarianism put forth blossoms. The poets, of course, had to make studies of their own, to decipher manuscripts, learn Old English, visit ruins, collect ballads and ancient armor, familiarize themselves with terms of heraldry, architecture, chivalry, ecclesiology and feudal law, and in other such ways inform and stimulate their imaginations. It was many years before the joint labors of scholars and poets had reconstructed an image of medieval society, sharp enough in outline and brilliant enough in color to impress itself upon the general public. Scott, indeed, was the first to popularize romance; mainly, no doubt, because of the greater power and fervor of his imagination; but also, in part, because an ampler store of materials had been already accumulated when he began work. He had fed on Percy's "Reliques" in boyhood; through Coleridge, his verse derives from Chatterton; and the line of Gothic romances which starts with "The Castle of Otranto" is remotely responsible for "Ivanhoe" and "The Talisman."

But Scott too was, like Percy and Walpole, a virtuoso

and collector; and the vast apparatus of notes and introductory matter in his metrical tales, and in the Waverley novels, shows how necessary it was for the romantic poet to be his own antiquary. As was to be expected, the zeal of the first romanticists was not always a zeal according to knowledge, and the picture of the Middle Age which they painted was more of a caricature than a portrait. A large share of medieval literature was inaccessible to the general reader. Much more of it was in old and rare printed copies, broadsides and black-letter folios, the treasure of great libraries and of jealously hoarded private collections. Much was in dialects little understood-forgotten forms of speech-Old French, Middle High German, Old Norse, medieval Latin, the ancient Erse and Cymric tongues, Anglo-Saxon. As such there was an almost total lack of apparatus for the study of this literature. Helps were needed in the shape of modern reprints of scarce texts, bibliographies, critical editions, translations, literary histories and manuals, glossaries of archaic words, dictionaries and grammars of obsolete languages. These were gradually supplied by working specialists in different fields of investigation. Every side of medieval life has received illustration in its turn.

Works like Tyrwhitt's edition of Chaucer (1775-78); the collections of mediaeval romances by Ellis (1805), Ritson (1802), and Weber (1810); Nares' and Halliwell's "Archaic Glossary" (1822-46), Carter's "Specimens of Ancient Sculpture and Paintings" (1780-94), Scott's "Demonology and Witchcraft" (1830), Hallam's "Middle Ages" (1818), Meyrick's "Ancient Armour" (1824), Lady Guest's "Mabinogion" (1838), the publications of numberless individual scholars and of learned societies like the Camden, the Spenser, the Percy, the Chaucer, the Early English Text, the Roxburgh Club,—to mention only English examples, taken at random and separated from each other by wide intervals of time,—are instances of the labors by which mediaeval life has been made familiar to all who might choose to make acquaintance with it.

It is worth mentioning that the history of romanticism, after the impulse had once been given, is little else than a record or the steps by which, one after another, new features of that vast and complicated scheme of things which we loosely call the Middle Ages were brought to light and made available as literary material. The picture was constantly having fresh details added to it, nor is there any reason to believe that it is finished yet. Some of the finest pieces of mediaeval work have only within the last few years been brought to the attention of the general reader; e.g., the charming old French story in prose and verse, "Aucassin et Nicolete," and the fourteenth-century English poem, "The Perle."

The future holds still other phases of romanticism in reserve; the Middle Age seems likely to be as inexhaustible in novel sources of inspiration as classical antiquity has already proved to be. The past belongs to the poet no less than the present, and a great part of the literature of every generation will always be retrospective. The tastes and preferences of the individual artist will continue to find a wide field for selection in the rich quarry of Christian and feudal Europe. It is not a little odd that the book which first aroused, in modern Europe, an interest in Norse mythology should have been written by a Frenchman. "Introduction à l'Histoire de Dannemarc," published in 1755 by Paul Henri Mallet, included also a translation of the first part of the Younger Edda, with an abstract of the second part and of the Elder Edda, and versions of several Runic poems. It was translated into English, in 1770, by Thomas Percy, the editor of the "Reliques," under the title, "Northern Antiquities; or a Description of the Manners, Customs, Religion, and Laws of the ancient Danes."

A German translation had appeared a few years earlier and had inspired the Schleswig-Holsteiner, Heinrich Wilhem von Gerstenberg, to compose his "Gedicht eines Skalden," which introduced the old Icelandic mythology into German poetry in 1766. Percy had published independently in

1763 "Five Pieces of Runic Poetry, translated from the Icelandic Language."

Gray did not wait for the English translation of Mallet's book. In a letter to Mason, dated in 1758, and inclosing some criticisims on the latter's "Caractacus" (then in MS.), he wrote, "I am pleased with the Gothic Elysium. Do you think I am ignorant about either that, or the hell before, or the twilight. I have been there and have seen it all in Mallet's 'Introduction to the History of Denmark' (French), and many other places." It is a far cry from Mallet's "System of Runic Mythology" to William Morris' "Sigurd the Volsung" (1877), but to Mallet belongs the credit of first exciting that interest in Scandinavian antiquity which has enriched the prose and poetry not only of England but of Europe in general. Gray refers to him in his notes on "The Descent of Odin," and his work continued to be popular authority on its subject for at least half a century. Scott cites it in his annotations on "The Lay of the Last Minstrel" (1805).

It is pertinent to note that Gray's studies in Runic literature took shape in "The Fatal Sisters" and "The Descent of Odin," written in 1761, published in 1768. These were paraphrases of two poems which Gray found in the "De Causis Contemnendae Mortis" (Copenhagen, 1689) of Thomas Bartholin, a Danish physician of the seventeenth century. The first of them describes the Valkyrie weaving the fates of the Danish and Irish warriors in the battle of Clontarf, fought in the eleventh century between Sigurd, Earl of Orkney, and Brian, King of Dublin; the second narrates the descent of Odin to Niflheimer, to inquire of Hela concerning the doom of Balder. Gray had designed these for the introductory chapter of his projected history of English poetry. He calls them imitations, which in fact they are, rather than literal renderings.

In spite of a tinge of eighteenth-century diction, and of one or two Shakspearian and Miltonic phrases, the translator succeeded fairly well in reproducing the wild air of his originals. His biographer, Mr. Gosse, promises that "the student will not fail . . . in the Gothic picturesqueness of 'The Descent of Odin,' to detect notes and phrases of a more delicate originality than are to be found even in his more famous writings; and will dwell with peculiar pleasure on those passages in which Gray freed himself of the trammels of an artificial and conventional taste, and prophesied of the new romantic age that was coming." Celtic antiquity shared with Gothic in this newly around interest. Here too, as in the phrase about "the stormy Hebrides," "Lycidas" seems to have furnished the spark that kindled the imaginations of the poets.

Another time, to illustrate the following suggestion: "I have frequently wondered that our modern writers have made so little use of the druidical times and the traditions of the old bards. . . Milton, we see, was sensible of the force of such imagery, as we may gather from this short but exquisite passage." As further illustrations of the poetic capabilities of similar themes, Warton gives a stanza from Gray's "Bard" and some lines from Gilbert West's "Institution of the Order of the Garter" which describe the ghosts of the Druids hovering about their ruined altars at Stonehenge:

"—Mysterious rows
Of rude enormous obelisks, that rise
Orb within orb, stupendous monuments
Of artless architecture, such as now
Oft-times amaze the wandering traveler,
By the pale moon discerned on Sarum's plain."

He then inserts two stanzas, in the Latin of Hickes' "Thesaurus," of an old Runic ode preserved by Olaus Wormius (Ole Worm) and adds an observation upon the Scandinavian heroes and their contempt of death. Druids and bards now begin to abound. Collins' "Ode on the Death of Mr. Thomson," e.g., commences with the line

"In yonder grave a Druid lies."

In his "Ode to Liberty," he alludes to the tradition that Mona, the druidic stronghold, was long covered with an enchantment of mist—work of an angry mermaid:

"Mona, once hid from those who search the main,
Where thousand elfin shapes abide."

Mason's "Caractacus" (1759) was a dramatic poem on the Greek model, with a chorus of British bards, and a principal Druid for choragus. The scene is the sacred grove in Mona. Mason got up with much care the description of druidic rites, such as the preparation of the adder-stone and the cutting of the mistletoe with a gold sickle, from Latin authorities like Pliny, Tacitus, Lucan, Strabo, and Suetonius. Joseph Warton commends highly the chorus on "Death" in this piece, as well as the chorus of bards at the end of West's "Institution of the Garter."

For the materials of his "Bard" Gray had to go no farther than historians and chroniclers such as Camden, Higden, and Matthew of Westminster, to all of whom he refers. Following a now discredited tradition, he represents the last survivor of the Welsh poetic guild, seated, harp in hand, upon a crag on the side of Snowdon, and denouncing judgment on Edward I, for the murder of his brothers in song. But in 1764 Gray was incited, by the publication of Dr. Evans' "Specimens," to attempt a few translations from the Welsh. The most considerable of these was "The Triumphs of Owen," published among Gray's collected poems in 1768. This celebrates the victory over the confederate fleets of Ireland, Denmark, and Normandy, won about 1160 by a prince of North Wales, Owen Ap Griffin, "the dragon son on Mona." The other fragments are brief but spirited versions of bardic songs in praise of fallen heroes: "Caràdòc," "Conan," and "The Death of Hoel." They were printed posthumously, though composed in 1764. The scholarship of the day was not always accurate in discriminating between ancient systems of religion, and Gray, in his letters to Mason in 1758, when "Caractacus" was still in the works, takes him to task for mixing the Gothic and Celtic mythologies. He instructs him that Woden and his Valhalla belong to "the doctrine of the Scalds, not of the Bards"; but admits that, "in that scarcity of Celtic ideas we labor under," it might be permissible to borrow from the Edda, "dropping, however, all mention of Woden and his Valkyrian virgins," and "without entering too minutely on particulars"; or "still better, to graft any wild picturesque fable, absolutely of one's own invention, upon the Druid stock."

But Gray had not scrupled to mix mythologies in "The Bard," thereby incurring Dr. Johnson's censure. "The weaving of the winding sheet he borrowed, as he owns, from the northern bards; but their texture, however, was very properly the work of female powers, as the art of spinning the thread of life in another mythology. Theft is always dangerous: Gray has made weavers of the slaughtered bards, by a fiction outrageous and incongruous." Indeed Mallet himself had a very confused notion of the relation of the Celtic to the Teutonic race. He speaks constantly of the old Scandinavians as Celts. Percy points out the difference, in the preface to his translation, and makes the necessary correction in the text, where the word Celtic occurs—usually by substituting "Gothic and Celtic" for the "Celtic" of the original.

Mason made his contribution to Runic literature, "Song of Harold the Valiant," a rather insipid versification of a passage from the "Knytlinga Saga," which had been rendered by Bartholin into Latin, from him into French by Mallet, and from Mallet into English prose by Percy. Mason designed it for insertion in the introduction to Gray's abortive history of English poetry.

The closing lines of Thomas Warton's sonnet "Written in a Blank Leaf of Dugdale's Monasticon"—a favorite with Charles Lamb—might have been written by Longfellow:

"Nor rough nor barren are the winding ways
Of hoar Antiquity, but strewn with flowers."

Joseph Warton's pretensions, as a poet, are much less than his younger brother's. Much of Thomas Warton's poetry, such as his facetiae in the "Oxford Sausage" and his "Triumph of Isis," had an academic flavor. So, too, with most of his annual laureate odes, "On his Majesty's Birthday," etc. Yet even these official and rather perfunctory performances testify to his fondness for what Scott calls "the memorials of our forefathers' piety or splendor." Thus, in the birthday odes for 1787-88, and the New Year ode for 1787, he pays a tribute to the ancient minstrels and to early laureates like Chaucer and Spenser, and celebrates "the Druid harp" sounding "through the gloom profound of forests hoar"; the fanes and castles built by the Normans; and the

"—bright hall where Odin's Gothic throne
With the broad blaze of brandished falchions shone."

But the most purely romantic of Thomas Warton's poems are "The Crusade" and "The Grave of King Arthur." The former is the song which

"The lion heart Plantagenet
Sang, looking through his prison-bars,"

when the minstrel Blondel came wandering in search of his captive king. The latter describes how Henry II., on his way to Ireland, was feasted at Cilgarran Castle, where the Welsh bards sang to him of the death of Arthur and his burial in Glastonbury Abbey. The following passage anticipates Scott:

"Illumining the vaulted roof,
A thousand torches flamed aloof;
From many cups, with golden gleam,

Sparkled the red metheglin's stres
To grace the gorgeous festival,
Along the lofty-windowed hall
The storied tapestry was hung;
With minstrelsy the rafters rung
Of harps that with reflected light
From the proud gallery glittered bright:
While gifted bards, a rival throng,
From distant Mona, nurse of song,
From Teivi fringed with umbrage brown,
From Elvy's vale and Cader's crown,
From many a shaggy precipice
That shades Ierne's hoarse abyss,
And many a sunless solitude
Of Radnor's inmost mountains rude,
To crown the banquet's solemn close
Themes of British glory chose."

Other poems of Thomas Warton touching upon his favorite studies are the "Ode Sent to Mr. Upton, on his Edition of the Faery Queene," the "Monody Written near Stratford-upon-Avon," the sonnets, "Written at Stonehenge," "To Mr. Gray," and "On King Arthur's Round Table," and the humorous epistle which he attributes to Thomas Hearne, the antiquary, denouncing the bishops for their recent order that fast-prayers should be printed in modern type instead of black letter, and pronouncing a curse upon the author of *"The Companion to the Oxford Guide Book"* for his disrespectful remarks about antiquaries.

"May'st thou pore in vain
For dubious doorways! May revengeful moths
Thy ledgers eat! May chronologic spouts

Retain no cipher legible! May crypts
Lurk undiscovered! Nor may'st thou spell the names
Of saints in storied windows, nor the dates
Of bells discover, nor the genuine site
Of abbots' pantries!"

Warton was a classical scholar and, like most of the forerunners of the romantic school, was a trifle shamefaced over his Gothic heresies. Sir Joshua Reynolds had supplied a painted window of classical design for New College, Oxford; and Warton, in some complimentary verses, professes that those "portraitures of Attic art" have won him back to the true taste; and prophesies that henceforth angels, apostles, saints, miracles, martyrdoms, and tales of legendary lore shall—

"No more the sacred window's round disgrace,
But yield to Grecian groups the shining space. . .
Thy powerful hand has broke the Gothic chain,
And brought my bosom back to truth again. . .
For long, enamoured of a barbarous age,
A faithless truant to the classic page—
Long have I loved to catch the simple chime
Of minstrel harps, and spell the fabling rime;
To view the festive rites, the knightly play,
That decked heroic Albion's elder day;
To mark the mouldering halls of barons bold,
And the rough castle, cast in giant mould;
With Gothic manners, Gothic arts explore,
And muse on the magnificence of yore.
But chief, enraptured have I loved to roam,
A lingering votary, the vaulted dome,
Where the tall shafts, that mount in massy pride,

Their mingling branches shoot from side to side;
Where elfin sculptors, with fantastic clew,
O'er the long roof their wild embroidery drew;
Where Superstition, with capricious hand,
In many a maze, the wreathëd window planned,
With hues romantic tinged the gorgeous pane,
To fill with holy light the wondrous fane."

The application of the word "romantic," in this passage, to the mediaeval art of glass-staining is significant. The revival of the art in our own day is due to the influence of the latest English school of romantic poetry and painting, and especially to William Morris. Warton's biographers track his passion for antiquity to the impression left upon his mind by a visit to Windsor Castle, when he was a boy. He used to spend his summers in wandering through abbeys and cathedrals.

He kept notes of his observations and is known to have begun a work on Gothic architecture, no trace of which, however, was found among his manuscripts. The Bodleian Library was one of his haunts, and he was frequently seen "surveying with quiet and rapt earnestness the ancient gateway of Magdalen College." He delighted in illuminated manuscripts and black-letter folios. In his "Observations on the Faëry Queene" he introduces a digression of twenty pages on Gothic architecture, and speaks lovingly of a "very curious and beautiful folio manuscript of the history of Arthur and his knights in the Ashmolean Museum at Oxford, written on vellum, with illuminated initials and head-pieces, in which we see the fashion of ancient armour, building, manner of tilting and other particulars."

Another very characteristic poem of Warton's is the "Ode Written at Vale-Royal Abbey in Cheshire," a monastery of Cistercian monks, founded by Edward I. This piece is saturated with romantic feeling and written in the stanza and manner of Gray's "Elegy," as will appear from a pair of stanzas, taken at random:

"By the slow clock, in stately-measured chime,
That from the messy tower tremendous tolled,
No more the plowman counts the tedious time,
Nor distant shepherd pens the twilight fold.
"High o'er the trackless heath at midnight seen,
No more the windows, ranged in array
(Where the tall shaft and fretted nook between
Thick ivy twines), the tapered rites betray."

It is a note of Warton's period that, though Fancy and the Muse survey the ruins of the abbey with pensive regret, "severer Reason"—the real eighteenth-century divinity—"scans the scene with philosophic ken," and—being a Protestant—reflects that, after all, the monastic houses were "Superstition's shrine" and their demolition was a good thing for Science and Religion.

The greatest service, however, that Thomas Warton rendered to the studies that he loved was his "History of English Poetry from the Twelfth to the Close of the Sixteenth Century." This was in three volumes, published respectively in 1774, 1777, and 1781. The fragment of a fourth volume was issued in 1790. A revised edition in four volumes was published in 1824, under the editorship of Richard Price, corrected, augmented, and annotated by Ritson, Douce, Park, Ashby, and the editor himself. In 1871 appeared a new revision (also in four volumes) edited by W. Carew Hazlitt, with many additions, by the editor and by well-known English scholars like Madden, Skeat, Furnivall, Morris, and Thomas and Aldis Wright. It should never be forgotten, in estimating the value of Warton's work, that he was a forerunner in this field. Much of his learning is out of date, and the modern editors of his history—Price and Hazlitt—seem to the discouraged reader to be chiefly engaged, in their footnotes and bracketed interpellations, in taking back statements that Warton had made in the text. The leading position, e.g., of his preliminary dissertation, "Of the Origin of Romantic Fiction in Europe"—deriving it from the Spanish Arabs—has long since been discredited. But Warton's learning was wide, if not exact; and it was not dry learning, but quickened by the spirit of a genuine man of letters. Therefore, in spite of its obsoleteness in matters of fact, his history remains readable, as a body of descriptive criticism, or a continuous literary essay. The best way to read it is to read it as it was written—in the original edition—disregarding the apparatus of notes, which modern scholars have accumulated about it, but remembering that it is no longer an authority and probably needs correcting on every page. Read thus, it is a thoroughly delightful book, "a classic in its way," as Lowell has said. Southey, too, affirmed that its publication formed an epoch in literary history; and that, with Percy's "Reliques," it had promoted, beyond any other work, the "growth of a better taste than had prevailed for the hundred years preceding."

> Gray had schemed a history of English poetry, but relinquished the design
>
> to Warton, to whom he communicated an outline of his own plan. The
>
> "Observations on English Metre" and the essay on the poet Lydgate, among
>
> Gray's prose remains, are apparently portions of this projected work.

Lowell, furthermore, pronounces Joseph Warton's "Essay on the Genius and Writings of Pope" (1756) "the earliest public official declaration of war against the reigning mode." The new school had its critics, as well as its poets, and the Wartons were more effective in the former capacity. The war thus opened was by no means as internecine as that waged by the French classicists and romanticists of 1830. It has never been possible to get up a very serious conflict in England, upon merely aesthetic grounds. Yet the same opposition existed. Warton's biographer tells us that the strictures made upon his essay were "powerful enough to damp the ardor of the essayist, who left his work in an imperfect state for the long space of twenty-six years," i.e., till 1782, when he published the second volume.

Both Wartons were personal friends of Dr. Johnson; they were members of the Literary Club and contributors to the Idler and the Adventurer. Thomas interested himself to get Johnson the Master's degree from Oxford, where the doctor made him a visit. Some correspondence between them is given in Boswell. Johnson maintained in public a respectful attitude toward the critical and historical work of the Wartons; but he had no sympathy with their antiquarian enthusiasm or their liking for old English poetry. In private he ridiculed Thomas' verses, and summed them up in the manner ensuing:

> "Whereso'er I turn my view,
> All is strange yet nothing new;
> Endless labor all along,
> Endless labor to be wrong;
> Phrase that time has flung away,
> Uncouth words in disarray,
> Tricked in antique ruff and bonnet,
> Ode and elegy and sonnet."

And although he added, "Remember that I love the fellow dearly, for all I laugh at him," this saving clause failed to soothe the poet's indignant breast, when he heard that the doctor had ridiculed his lines. An estrangement resulted which Johnson is said to have spoken of even with tears, saying "that Tom Warton was the only man of genius he ever knew who wanted a heart."

Goldsmith, too, belonged to the conservative party,

though Mr. Perry detects romantic touches in "The Deserted Village," such as the line,

> "Where wild Altama murmurs to their woe,"
>
> or
>
> "On Torno's cliffs or Pambamarca's side."

In his *"Enquiry into the Present State of Polite Learning"* (1759) Goldsmith pronounces the age one of literary decay; he deplores the vogue of blank verse—which he calls an "erroneous innovation"—and the "disgusting solemnity of manner" that it has brought into fashion. He complains of the revival of old plays upon the stage. "Old pieces are revived, and scarcely any new ones admitted. . . The public are again obliged to ruminate over those ashes of absurdity which were disgusting to our ancestors even in an age of ignorance. . . What must be done? Only sit down contented, cry up all that comes before us and advance even the absurdities of Shakspeare. Let the reader suspend his censure; I admire the beauties of this great father of our stage as much as they deserve, but could wish, for the honor of our country, and for his own too, that many of his scenes were forgotten. A man blind of one eye should always be painted in profile. Let the spectator who assists at any of these new revived pieces only ask himself whether he would approve such a performance, if written by a modern poet. I fear he will find that much of his applause proceeds merely from the sound of a name and an empty veneration for antiquity. In fact, the revival of those pieces of forced humor, far-fetched conceit and unnatural hyperbole which have been ascribed to Shakspeare, is rather gibbeting than raising a statue to his memory."

Goldsmith returned to the charge in "The Vicar of Wakefield" (1766), where Dr. Primrose, inquiring of the two London dames, "who were the present theatrical writers in vogue, who were the Drydens and Otways of the day," is surprised to learn that Dryden and Rowe are quite out of fashion, that taste has gone back a whole century, and that "Fletcher, Ben Jonson and all the plays of Shakspeare are the only things that go down." "How," cries the good vicar, "is it possible the present age can be pleased with that antiquated dialect, that obsolete humor, those overcharged characters which abound in the works you mention?"

Goldsmith's disgust with this affectation finds further vent in his "Life of Parnell" (1770). "He [Parnell] appears to me to be the last of that great school that had modeled itself upon the ancients, and taught English poetry to resemble what the generality of mankind have allowed to excel. . . His productions bear no resemblance to those tawdry things which it has, for some time, been the fashion to admire. . . His poetical language is not less correct than his subjects are pleasing. He found it at that period in which it was brought to its highest pitch of refinement; and ever since his time, it has been gradually debasing. It is, indeed, amazing, after what has been done by Dryden, Addison, and Pope, to improve and harmonize our native tongue, that their successors should have taken so much pains to involve it into pristine barbarity. These misguided innovators have not been content with restoring antiquated words and phrases, but have indulged themselves in the most licentious transpositions and the harshest constructions; vainly imagining that, the more their writings are unlike prose, the more they resemble poetry. They have adopted a language of their own, and call upon mankind for admiration. All those who do not understand them are silent; and those who make out their meaning are willing to praise, to show they understand."

This last sentence is a hit at the alleged obscurity of Gray's and Mason's odes.

To illustrate the growth of a retrospective habit in literature Perry quotes at length from an essay "On the Prevailing Taste for the Old English Poets," by Vicesimus

Knox, sometimes master of Tunbridge school, editor of "Elegant Extracts" and honorary doctor of the University of Pennsylvania. Knox's essays were written while he was an Oxford undergraduate, and published collectively in 1777. By this time the romantic movement was in full swing.

"The Castle of Otranto" and Percy's "Reliques" had been out more than ten years; many of the Rowley poems were in print; and in this very year, Tyrwhitt issued a complete edition of them, and Warton published the second volume of his "History of English Poetry." Chatterton and Percy are both mentioned by Knox. "The antiquarian spirit," he writes, "which was once confined to inquiries concerning the manners, the buildings, the records, and the coins of the ages that preceded us, has now extended itself to those poetical compositions which were popular among our forefathers, but which have gradually sunk into oblivion through the decay of language and the prevalence of a correct and polished taste. Books printed in the black letter are sought for with the same avidity with which the English antiquary peruses a monumental inscription, or treasures up a Saxon piece of money.

The popular ballad, composed by some illiterate minstrel, and which has been handed down by tradition for several centuries, is rescued from the hands of the vulgar, to obtain a place in the collection of the man of taste. Verses which, a few years past, were thought worthy the attention of children only, or of the lowest and rudest orders, are now admired for that artless simplicity which once obtained the name of coarseness and vulgarity." Early English poetry, continues the essayist, "has had its day, and the antiquary must not despise us if we cannot peruse it with patience. He who delights in all such reading as is never read, may derive some pleasure from the singularity of his taste, but he ought still to respect the judgment of mankind, which has consigned to oblivion the works which he admires. While he pores unmolested on Chaucer, Gower, Lydgate, and Occleve, let him not censure our obstinacy in adhering to Homer, Virgil, Milton, and Pope. . . Notwithstanding the incontrovertible merit of many of our ancient relics of poetry, I believe it may be doubted whether any one of them would be tolerated as the production of a modern poet. As a good imitation of the ancient manner, it would find its admirers; but, considered independently, as an original, it would be thought a careless, vulgar, inartificial composition. There are few who do not read Dr. Percy's own pieces, and those of other late writers, with more pleasure than the oldest ballad in the collection of that ingenious writer." Mr. Percy quotes another paper of Knox in which he divides the admirers of English poetry into two parties: "On one side are the lovers and imitators of Spenser and Milton; and on the other, those of Dryden, Boileau, and Pope"; in modern phrase, the romanticists and the classicists.

Joseph Warton's *"Essay on Pope"* was an attempt to fix its subject's rank among English poets. Following the discursive method of Thomas Warton's *"Observations on the Faerie Queen,"* it was likewise an elaborate commentary on all of Pope's poems seriatim. Every point was illustrated with abundant learning, and there were digressions amounting to independent essays on collateral topics: one, e.g., on Chaucer, one on early French Metrical romances; another on Gothic architecture: another on the new school of landscape gardening, in which Walpole's essay and Mason's poem are quoted with approval, and mention is made of the Leasowes. The book was dedicated to Young; and when the second volume was published in 1782, the first was reissued in a revised form and introduced by a letter to the author from Tyrwhitt, who writes that, under the shelter of Warton's authority, "one may perhaps venture to avow an opinion that poetry is not confined to rhyming couplets, and that its greatest powers are not displayed in prologues and epilogues."

Every scholar may think Warton's estimate of Pope

quite high enough. He places him, to be sure, in the second rank of poets, below Spenser, Shakspeare, and Milton, yet next to Milton and above Dryden; and he calls the reign of Queen Anne the great age of English poetry. Yet if it be recollected that the essay was published only twelve years after Pope's death, and at a time when he was still commonly held to be, if not the greatest poet, at least the greatest artist in verse, that England had ever produced, it will be seen that Warton's opinions might well be thought revolutionary, and his challenge to the critics a bold one. These opinions can be best exhibited by quoting a few passages from his book, not consecutive, but taken here and there as best suits the purpose.

"The sublime and the pathetic are the two chief nerves of all genuine poesy. What is there transcendently sublime or pathetic in Pope?. . . He early left the more poetical provinces of his art, to become a moral, didactic, and satiric poet. . . And because I am, perhaps, unwilling to speak out in plain English, I will adopt the following passage of Voltaire, which, in my opinion, as exactly characteristizes Pope as it does his model, Boileau, for whom it was originally designed. 'Incapable peut-être du sublime qui élève l'áme, et du sentiment qui l'attendrit, mais fait pour éclairer ceux à qui la nature accorda l'un et l'autre; laborieux, sévère, précis, pur, harmonieux, il devint enfin le poëte de la Raison.'. . . A clear head and acute understanding are not sufficient alone to make a poet; the most solid observations on human life, expressed with the utmost elegance and brevity, are morality and not poetry. . . It is a creative and glowing imagination, acer spiritus ac vis, and that alone, that can stamp a writer with this exalted and very uncommon character."

In fact, Warton believes that Pope's projected epic on Brutus, the legendary found of Britain, "would have more resembled the 'Henriade' than the 'Iliad,' or even the 'Gierusalemme Liberata'; that it would have appeared (if this scheme had been executed) how much, and for what reasons, the man that is skillful in painting modern life, and the most secret foibles and follies of his contemporaries, is, THEREFORE, disqualified for representing the ages of heroism, and that simple life which alone epic poetry can gracefully describe. . . Wit and satire are transitory and perishable, but nature and passion are eternal." The largest portion of Pope's work, says the author's closing summary, "is of the didactic, moral, and satiric kind; and consequently not of the most poetic species of poetry; when it is manifest that good sense and judgment were his characteristical excellencies, rather than fancy and invention. . . He stuck to describing modern manners; but those manners, because they are familiar, uniform, artificial, and polished, are in their very nature, unfit for any lofty effort of the Muse. He gradually became one of the most correct, even, and exact poets that ever wrote. . . Whatever poetical enthusiasm he actually possessed, he withheld and stifled. The perusal of him affects not our minds with such strong emotions as we feel from Homer and Milton; so that no man of a true poetical spirit is master of himself while he reads them. . . He who would think the 'Faerie Queene,' 'Palamon and Arcite,' the 'Tempest' or 'Comus,' childish and romantic might relish Pope. Surely it is no narrow and niggardly encomium to say, he is the great poet of Reason, the first of ethical authors in verse."

It is pertinent to note that to illustrate Pope's inferiority in the poetry of nature and passion, Warton quotes freely by way of contrast, not only from Spenser and Milton, but from such contemporaries of his own as Thomson, Akenside, Gray, Collins, Dyer, Mason, West, Shenstone, and Bedingfield. He complains that Pope's "Pastorals" contains no new image of nature, and his "Windsor Forest" no local color; while "the scenes of Thomson are frequently as wild and romantic as those of Salvator Rosa, varied with precipices and torrents and 'castled cliffs' and deep valleys, with piny mountains and the gloomiest caverns." "When Gray published his exquisite ode on Eton College . . . little notice was taken of it; but I suppose no critic can be found that will not place it far above Pope's 'Pastorals.'"

A few additional passages will serve to show that this critic's literary principles, in general, were consciously and polemically romantic. Thus he pleads for the mot précis—that shibboleth of the nineteenth-century romanticists—for "natural, little circumstances" against "those who are fond of generalities"; for the "lively painting of Spenser and Shakspeare," as contrasted with the lack of picturesqueness and imagery in Voltaire's "Henriade." He praises "the fashion that has lately obtained, in all the nations of Europe, of republishing and illustrating their old poets."

"What! Did Milton contribute nothing to the harmony and extent of our language?. . . Surely his verses vary and resound as much, and display as much majesty and energy, as any that can be found in Dryden. And we will venture to say that he that studies Milton attentively, will gain a truer taste for genuine poetry than he that forms himself on French writers and their followers." Elsewhere he expresses a preference for blank verse over rhyme, in long poems on subjects of a dignified kind.

"It is perpetually the nauseous cant of the French critics, and of their advocates and pupils, that the English writers are generally incorrect. If correctness implies an absence of petty faults, this perhaps may be granted; if it means that, because their tragedians have avoided the irregularities of Shakspeare, and have observed a juster economy in their fables, therefore the 'Athalia,' for instance, is preferable to 'Lear,' the notion is groundless and absurd. Though the 'Henriade' should be allowed to be free from any very gross absurdities, yet who will dare to rank it with the 'Paradise Lost'?. . . In our own country the rules of the drama were never more completely understood than at present; yet what uninteresting, though faultless, tragedies have we lately seen!. . . Whether or no the natural powers be not confined and debilitated by that timidity and caution which is occasioned by a rigid regard to the dictates of art; or whether that philosophical, that geometrical and systematical spirit so much in vogue, which has spread itself from the sciences even into polite literature, by consulting only reason, has not diminished and destroyed sentiment, and made our poets write from and to the head rather than the heart; or whether, lastly, when just models, from which the rules have necessarily been drawn, have once appeared, succeeding writers, by vainly and ambitiously striving to surpass those . . . do not become stiff and forced." One of these uninteresting, though faultless tragedies was "Cato," which Warton pronounces a "sententious and declamatory drama" filled with "pompous Roman sentiments," but wanting action and pathos. He censures the tameness of Addison's "Letter from Italy." "With what flatness and unfeelingness has he spoken of statuary and painting! Raphael never received a more phlegmatic eulogy." He refers on the other hand to Gray's account of his journey to the Grande Chartreuse, as worthy of comparison with one of the finest passages in the "Epistle of Eloisa to Abelard."

No doubt, this mention of Addison recalls a very instructive letter of Gray on the subject of poetic style. The romanticists loved a rich diction, and the passage might be taken as an anticipatory defense of himself against Wordsworth's strictures in the preface to the "Lyrical Ballads." "The language of the age," wrote Gray, "is never the language of poetry, except among the French, whose verse . . . differs in nothing from prose. Our poetry has a language peculiar to itself; to which almost everyone that has written has added something, by enriching it with foreign idioms and derivatives; nay, sometimes words of their own composition or invention. Shakspeare and Milton have been great creators in this way . . . our language has an undoubted right to words of an hundred years old, provided antiquity have not rendered them unintelligible. In truth Shakspeare's language is one of his principal beauties; and he has no less advantage over your Addisons and Rowes in this, than in those other great excellencies you mention. Every word in him is a picture."

He then quotes a passage from "Richard III.," and continues, "Pray put me the following lines into the tongue of our modern dramatics. To me they appear untranslatable, and if this be the case, our language is greatly degenerated."

Warton further protests against the view which ascribed the introduction of true taste in literature to the French. "Shakspeare and Milton imitated the Italians and not the French." He recommends also the reintroduction of the preternatural into poetry. There are some, he says, who think that poetry has suffered by becoming too rational, deserting fairyland, and laying aside "descriptions of magic and enchantment," and he quotes, à propos of this the famous stanza about the Hebrides in "The Castle of Indolence." The false refinement of the French has made them incapable of enjoying "the terrible graces of our irregular Shakspeare, especially in his scenes of magic and incantations. These Gothic charms are in truth more striking to the imagination than the classical. The magicians of Ariosto, Tasso, and Spenser have more powerful spells than those of Apollonius, Seneca, and Lucan. The enchanted forest of Ismeni is more awfully and tremendously poetical than even the grove which Caesar orders to be cut down in Lucan (i. iii. 400), which was so full of terrors that, at noonday or midnight, the priest himself dared not approach it—

> "'Dreading the demon of the grove to meet.'
>
> "Who that sees the sable plumes waving on the prodigious helmet in the
>
> Castle of Otranto, and the gigantic arm on the top of the great
>
> staircase, is not more affected than with the paintings of Ovid and

> Apuleius? What a group of dreadful images do we meet with in the Edda!
>
> The Runic poetry abounds in them. Such is Gray's thrilling Ode on the
>
> 'Descent of Odin.'"

Warton predicts that Pope's fame as a poet will ultimately rest on his "Windsor Forest," his "Epistle of Eloisa to Abelard," and "The Rape of the Lock." To this prophecy time has already, in part, given the lie. Warton preferred "Windsor Forest" and "Eloisa" to the "Moral Essays" because they belonged to a higher kind of poetry. Posterity likes the "Moral Essays" better because they are better of their kind. They were the natural fruit of Pope's genius and of his time, while the others were artificial. We can go to Wordsworth for nature, to Byron for passion, and to a score of poets for both, but Pope remains unrivaled in his peculiar field. In other words, we value what is characteristic in the artist; the one thing which he does best, the precise thing which he can do and no one else can.

6

The Landscape Poets

Romanticism largely began as a reaction against the prevailing Enlightenment ideals of the day. Inevitably, the characterization of a broad range of contemporaneous poets and poetry under the single unifying name can be viewed more as an exercise in historical compartmentalization than an attempt to capture the essence of the actual 'movement'.

Indeed, the term "Romanticism" did not arise until the Victorian period. Nonetheless, poets such as William Wordsworth were actively engaged in trying to create a new kind of poetry that emphasized intuition over reason and the pastoral over the urban, often eschewing modern forms and language in an effort to use 'new' language. Wordsworth himself in the Preface to his and Coleridge's *Lyrical Ballads* defined good poetry as "the spontaneous overflow of powerful feelings," though in the same sentence he goes on to clarify this statement by asserting that nonetheless any poem of value must still be composed by a man "possessed of more than usual organic sensibility [who has] also thought long and deeply".

Thus, though many people seize unfairly upon the notion of spontaneity in Romantic Poetry, one must realize that the movement was still greatly concerned with the pain of composition, of translating these emotive responses into the form of Poetry. Indeed, Samuel Taylor Coleridge, another prominent Romantic poet and critic in his *On*

Poesy or Art sees art as "the mediatress between, and reconciler of nature and man". Such an attitude reflects what might be called the dominant theme of Romantic Poetry: the filtering of natural emotion through the human mind in order to create art, coupled with an awareness of the duality created by such a process.

Professor McClintock says, that the "beginning and presence of a creative, romantic movement is almost always shown by the love, study, and interpretation of physical nature." Why this should be true, at all events of the romantic movement that began in the eighteenth century, is obvious enough. Ruskin and Leslie Stephen have already been quoted, as witnesses to the fact that naturalism and romanticism had a common root: the desire, namely, to escape into the fresh air and into freer conditions, from a literature which dealt, in a strictly regulated way, with the indoor life of a highly artificial society. The pastoral had ceased to furnish any relief. Professing to chant the praises of innocence and simplicity, it had become itself utterly unreal and conventional, in the hands of cockneys like Philips and Pope. When the romantic spirit took possession of the poetry of nature, it manifested itself in a passion for wildness, grandeur, solitude. Of this there was as yet comparatively little even in the verse of Thomson, Shenstone, Akenside, and Dyer.

There is nothing necessarily romantic in literature that concerns itself with rural life or natural scenery. Still the work of these pioneers in the "return to nature" represents the transition, and must be taken into account in any complete history of the romantic movement. The first two, as we have seen, were among the earliest Spenserians: Dyer was a landscape painter, as well as a poet; and Shenstone was one of the best of landscape gardeners. But it is the beginnings that are important. It will be needless to pursue the history of nature poetry into its later developments; needless to review the writings of Cowper and Crabbe, for example,—neither of whom was romantic in any sense,—or even of Wordsworth, the spirit of whose art, as a whole, was far from romantic. Before taking up the writers above named, one by one, it will be well to notice the general change in the forms of verse, which was an outward sign of the revolution in poetic feeling. The imitation of Spenser was only one instance of a readiness to lay aside the heroic couplet in favor of other kinds which it had displaced, and in the interests of greater variety. "During the twenty-five years," says Mr. Goss, "from the publication of Thomson's 'Spring' in 1726, to that of Gray's 'Elegy' in 1751, the nine or ten leading poems or collections of verse which appeared were all of a new type; somber, as a rule, certainly stately, romantic in tone to the extreme, prepared to return, ignorantly indeed, but with respect, to what was 'Gothic' in manners, architecture, and language; all showing a more or less vague aspiration towards the nature, and not one composed in the heroic couplet hitherto so vigorously imposed on serious verse.

'The Seasons,' 'Night Thoughts' and 'The Grave' are written in blank verse: 'The Castle of Indolence' and 'The Schoolmistress' in Spenserian stanza; 'The Spleen' and 'Grongar Hill' in octosyllabics, while the early odes of Gray and those of Collins are composed in a great variety of simple but novel lyric measures." The only important writer who had employed blank verse in undramatic poetry between the publication of "Paradise Regained" in 1672, and Thomson's "Winter" in 1726, was John Philips.

In the brief prefatory note to "Paradise Lost," the poet of "L'Allegro" and "Il Penseroso," forgetting or disdaining the graces of his youthful muse, had spoken of rhyme as "the invention of a barbarous age," as "a thing trivial and of no true musical delight." Milton's example, of course, could not fail to give dignity and authority to the majestic rhythm that he had used; and Philips' mock-heroic "The Splendid Shilling" (1701), his occasional piece, "Blenheim" (1705), and his Georgic "Cyder" (1706), were all avowed imitation of Milton.

But the well-nigh solitary character of Philips' experiments was recognized by Thomson, in his allusion to the last-named poem:

> "Philips, Pomona's bard, the second thou
> Who nobly durst, in rime-unfettered verse,
> With British freedom sing the British song."

Philips' imitations of Milton, Johnson said that if the latter "had written after the improvements made by Dryden, it is reasonable to believe he would have admitted a more pleasing modulation of numbers into his work." Johnson hated Adam Smith, but when Boswell mentioned that Smith, in his rhetorical lectures at Glasgow University, had given the preference to rhyme over blank verse, the doctor exclaimed, "Sir, I was once in company with Smith and we did not take to each other; but had I known that he loved rhyme as much as you tell me he does, I should have hugged him."

It is noteworthy that 1725 James Thomson, a young Scotchman, came to London to push his literary fortunes. His countryman, David Malloch,—or Mallet, as he called himself in England,—at that time private tutor in the family of the Duke of Montrose, procured Thomson introductions into titled society, and helped him to bring out "Winter," the first installment of "The Seasons," which was published in 1726. Thomson's friend and biographer (1762) the Rev. Patrick Murdoch, says that the poem was "no sooner read than universally admired; those only excepted who had not been used to feel, or to look for anything in poetry beyond a point of satirical or epigrammatic wit, a smart antithesis richly trimmed with rhyme."

This is a palpable hit at the stronger contrast than between Thomson and Pope, not alone in subject and feeling, but in diction and verse. Thomson's style is florid and luxuriant, his numbers flowing and diffuse, while Pope had wonted the English ear to the extreme of compression in both language and meter. Pope is among the most quotable of poets, while Thomson's long poem, in spite of its enduring popularity, has contributed but a single phrase to the stock of current quotation: "To teach the young idea how to shoot."

"Winter" was followed by "Summer" in 1727, "Spring" in 1728, and the completed "Seasons" in 1730. Thomson made many changes and additions in subsequent editions. The original "Seasons" contained only 3902 lines (exclusive of the "Hymn"), while the author's final revision of 1746 gave 5413. One proof that "The Seasons" was the work of a fresh and independent genius is afforded by the many imitations to which it soon gave birth. In Germany, a passage from Brockes' translation (1745) was set to music by Haydn. J. P. Uz (1742) and Wieland each produced a "Frühling," in Thomson's manner; but the most distinguished of his German disciples was Ewald Christian von Kleist, whose "Fruhling" (1749) was a description of a country walk in spring, in 460 hexameter lines, accompanied, as in Thomson's "Hymn," with a kind of "Gloria in excelsis," to the creator of nature.

"The Seasons" was translated into French by Madame Bontemps in 1759, and called forth, among other imitations, "Les Saisons" of Saint Lambert, 1769 (revised and extended in 1771.) In England, Thomson's influence naturally manifested itself less in direct imitations of the scheme of his poem than in the contagion of his manner, which pervades the work of many succeeding poets, such as Akenside, Armstrong, Dyer, Somerville and Mallet.

"There was hardly one verse writer of any eminence," says Gosse, "from 1725-50, who was not in some manner guided or biased by Thomson, whose genius is to this day fertile in English literature." We have grown so accustomed to a more intimate treatment and a more spiritual interpretation of nature, that we are perhaps too apt to undervalue Thomson's simple descriptive or pictorial method.

Compared with Wordsworth's mysticism, with Shelley's passionate pantheism, with Byron's romantic gloom in presence of the mountains and the sea, with Keats' joyous re-creation of mythology, with Thoreau's Indian-like approach to the innermost arcana—with a dozen other moods familiar to the modern mind—it seems to us unimaginative. Thomson has been likened, as a colorist, to Rubens; and possibly the glow, the breadth, and the vital energy of his best passages, as of Rubens' great canvases, leave our finer perceptions untouched, and we ask for something more esoteric, more intense.

Still there are permanent and solid qualities in Thomson's landscape art, which can give delight even now to an unspoiled taste. To a reader of his own generation, "The Seasons" must have come as the revelation of a fresh world of beauty. Such passages as those which describe the first spring showers, the thunderstorm in summer, the trout-fishing, the sheep-washing, and the terrors of the winter night, were not only strange to the public of that day, but were new in English poetry. That the poet was something of a naturalist, who wrote lovingly and with his "eye upon the object," is evident from a hundred touches, like "auriculas with shining meal";

"The yellow wall-flower stained with iron brown;"

or,

"The bittern knows his time, with bill engulfed,
To shake the sounding marsh."

Thomson's scenery was genuine. His images of external nature are never false and seldom vague, like Pope's. In a letter to Lyttelton, he speaks of "the Muses of the great simple country, not the little fine-lady Muses of Richmond Hill." His delineations, if less sharp and finished in detail than Cowper's, have greater breadth. Coleridge's comparison of the two poets is well known: "The love of nature seems to have led Thomson to a cheerful religion, and a gloomy religion to have led Cowper to a love of nature. . . In chastity of diction and the harmony of blank verse, Cowper leaves Thomson immeasurably below him; yet I still feel the latter to have been the born poet."

"That entire prospect," says Miller,—"one of the finest in England, and eminently characteristic of what is best in English scenery—enabled me to understand what I had used to deem a peculiarity—in some measure a defect—in the landscapes of the poet Thomson. It must have often struck the Scotch reader that, in dealing with very extended prospects, he rather enumerates than describes. His pictures are often mere catalogues, in which single words stand for classes of objects, and in which the entire poetry seems to consist in an overmastering sense of vast extent, occupied by amazing multiplicity. . . Now the prospect from the hill at Hagley furnished me with the true explanation of this enumerative style. Measured along the horizon, it must, on the lowest estimate, be at least fifty miles in longitudinal extent; measured laterally, from the spectator forwards, at least twenty. . . The real area must rather exceed than fall short of a thousand square miles: the fields into which it is laid out are small, scarcely averaging a square furlong in superficies. . . With these there are commixed innumerable cottages, manor-houses, villages, towns. Here the surface is dimpled by unreckoned hollows; there fretted by uncounted mounds; all is amazing, overpowering multiplicity—a multiplicity which neither the pen nor the pencil can adequately express; and so description, in even the hands of a master, sinks into mere enumeration. The picture becomes a catalogue."

Wordsworth pronounced "The Seasons" "a work of inspiration," and said that much of it was "written from himself, and nobly from himself," but complained that the style was vicious. Thomson's diction is, in truth, not always worthy of his poetic feeling and panoramic power over landscape. It is academic and often tumid and wordy, abounding in Latinisms like effusive, precipitant, irriguous, horrific, turgent, amusive. The lover who hides by the stream where his mistress is bathing—that celebrated "serio-comic bathing"—is described as "the latent Damon"; and when the poet advises against the use of worms for trout bait, he puts it thus:

> "But let not on your hook the tortured worm
> Convulsive writhe in agonizing folds," etc.

The poets had now begun to withdraw from town and go out into the country, but in their retirement to the sylvan shades they were accompanied sometimes, indeed, by Milton's "mountain nymph, sweet Liberty," but quite as frequently by Shenstone's nymph, "coy Elegance," who kept reminding them of Vergil.

Thomson's blank verse, although, as Coleridge says, inferior to Cowper's, is often richly musical and with an energy unborrowed of Milton—as Cowper's is too apt to be, at least in his translation of Homer. Mr. Saintsbury detects a mannerism in the verse of "The Seasons," which he illustrates by citing three lines with which the poet "caps the climax of three several descriptive passages, all within the compass of half a dozen pages," viz.:

> "And Egypt joys beneath the spreading wave."
> "And Mecca saddens at the long delay."
> "And Thule bellows through her utmost isles."

It would be easy to add many other instances of this type of climacteric line, e.g. ("Summer," 859),

> "And Ocean trembles for his green domain."

For the blank verse of "The Seasons" is a blank verse which has been passed through the strainer of the heroic couplet. Though Thomson, in the flow and continuity of his measure, offers, as has been said, the greatest contrast to Pope's system of versification; yet wherever he seeks to be nervous, his modulation reminds one more of Pope's antithetical trick than of Shakspeare's or Milton's freer structure. For instance ("Spring," 1015):

"Fills every sense and pants in every vein."

or (Ibid. *1104):*

"Flames through the nerves and boils along the veins."

To relieve the monotony of a descriptive poem, the author introduced moralizing digressions: advice to the husbandman and the shepherd after the manner of the "Georgics"; compliments to his patrons, like Lyttelton, Bubb Dodington, and the Countess of Hertford; and sentimental narrative episodes, such as the stories of Damon and Musidora, and Celadon and Amelia in "Summer," and of Lavinia and Palemon in "Autumn"; while ever and anon his eye extensive roamed over the phenomena of nature in foreign climes, the arctic night, the tropic summer, etc. Wordsworth asserts that these sentimental passages "are the parts of the work which were probably most efficient in first recommending the author to general notice."

They strike us now as insipid enough. But many coming attitudes cast their shadows before across the page of "The Seasons." Thomson's denunciation of the slave trade, and of cruelty to animals, especially the caging of birds and the coursing of hares; his preference of country to town; his rhapsodies on domestic love and the innocence of the Golden Age; his contrast between the misery of the poor and the heartless luxury of the rich; all these features of the poem foretoken the sentimentalism of Sterne and Goldsmith, and the humanitarianism of Cowper and Burns. They anticipate, in particular, that half affected itch of simplicity which titillated the sensibilities of a corrupt and artificial society in the writings of Rousseau and the idyllic pictures of Bernardin de St. Pierre's "Paul and Virginia." Thomson went so far in this vein as to decry the use of animal food in a passage which recalls Goldsmith's stanza:

"No flocks that range the valley free
To slaughter I condemn:
Taught by the power that pities me,
I learn to pity them."

This sort of thing was in the air. Pope was not a sentimental person, yet even Pope had written

"The lamb thy riot dooms to bleed to-day,
Had he thy reason, would he skip and play?
Pleased to the last, he crops the flowery food.
And licks the hand just raised to shed his blood."

It does not appear that Thomson was personally averse to a leg of mutton. His denunciations of luxury, and his praise of early rising and cold bathing sound rather hollow from the lips of a bard—"more fat than bard beseems"-who used to lie abed till noon, and who, as Savage told Johnson, "was perhaps never in cold water in his life." Johnson reports, not without some spice of malice, that the Countess of Hertford, "whose practice it was to invite every summer some poet into the country, to hear her verses and assist her studies," extended this courtesy to Thomson, "who took more delight in carousing with Lord Hertford and his friends than assisting her ladyship's poetical operations, and therefore never received another summons."

The romantic note is not absent from "The Seasons," but it is not prominent. Thomson's theme was the changes of the year as they affect the English landscape, a soft, cultivated landscape of lawns, gardens, fields, orchards, sheep-walks, and forest preserves. Only now and then that attraction toward the savage, the awful, the mysterious, the primitive, which marks the romantic mood in naturalistic poetry, shows itself in touches like these.

"High from the summit of a craggy cliff,
Hung o'er the deep, such as amazing frowns

On utmost Kilda's shore, whose lonely race
Reigns the setting sun to Indian worlds."
"Or where the Northern Ocean, in vast whirls,
Boils round the naked, melancholy isles
Of farthest Thule, and the Atlantic surge
Pours in among the stormy Hebrides."

The Western Islands appear to have had a peculiar fascination for Thomson. The passages above quoted, and the stanza from "The Castle of Indolence," cited on page 94, gave Collins the clew for his "Ode on the Superstitions of the Scottish Highlands," which contained, says Lowell, the whole romantic school in the germ. Thomason had perhaps found the embryon atom in Milton's "stormy Hebrides," in "Lycidas," whose echo is prolonged in Wordsworth's "Solitary Reaper"—

"Breaking the silence of the seas
Among the farthest Hebrides."

Even Pope—he had a soul—was not unsensitive to this, as witness his

"Loud as the wolves, on Orcas' stormy steep,
Howl to the roarings of the Northern deep."

The melancholy which Victor Hugo pronounces a distinguishing badge of romantic art, and which we shall see gaining more and more upon English poetry as the century advanced, is also discernible in "The Seasons" in a passage like the following:

"O bear me then to vast embowering shades,
To twilight groves and visionary vales,
To weeping grottos and prophetic glooms;
Where angel-forms athwart the solemn dusk
Tremendous sweep, or seem to sweep along;

And voices more than human, through the void,
Deep-sounding, seize the enthusiastic ear;"

or this, which recalls "Il Penseroso":

"Now all amid the rigors of the year,
In the wild depth of winter, while without
The ceaseless winds blow ice, be my retreat
Between the groaning forest and the shore,
Beat by the boundless multitude of waves,
A rural, sheltered, solitary scene;
Where ruddy fire and beaming tapers join
To cheer the gloom. There studious let me sit
And hold high converse with the mighty dead."

The revival again, of the preternatural and of popular superstitions as literary material, after a rationalizing and skeptical age, is signalized by such a passage as this:

"Onward they pass, o'er many a panting height,
And valley sunk and unfrequented, where
At fall of eve the fairy people throng,
In various game and revelry to pass
The summer night, as village stories tell.
But far around they wander from the grave
Of him whom his ungentle fortune urged
Against his own sad breast to life the hand
Of impious violence. The lonely tower
Is also shunned, whose mournful chambers hold,
So night-struck fancy dreams, the yelling ghost."

It may not be uninstructive to note the occurrence of the word romantic at several points in the poem:

"glimmering shades and sympathetic glooms, Where the dim umbrage o'er the falling stream Romantic hangs."

This is from a passage in which romantic love once more comes back into poetry, after its long eclipse; and in which the lover is depicted as wandering abroad at "pensive dusk," or by moonlight, through groves and along brooksides. The word is applied likewise to clouds, "rolled into romantic shapes, the dream of waking fancy"; and to the scenery of Scotland—"Caledonia in romantic view." In a subtler way, the feeling of such lines as these is romantic:

> "Breathe your still song into the reaper's heart,
> As home he goes beneath the joyous moon;"

or these, of the comparative lightness of the summer night:

> "A faint, erroneous ray,
> Glanced from the imperfect surfaces of things,
> Flings half an image on the straining eye."

In a letter to Stonehewer (June 29, 1760), Gray comments thus upon a passage from Ossian:

> "'Ghosts ride on the tempest to-night: Sweet is their voice between the gusts of wind: Their songs are of other worlds.'
>
> "Did you never observe (while rocking winds are piping loud) that pause, as the gust is re-collecting itself, and rising upon the ear in a shrill and plaintive note, like the soul of an Aeolian harp? I do assure you, there is nothing in the world so like the voice of a spirit. Thomson had an ear sometimes; he was not deaf to this, and has described it gloriously, but given it another, different turn, and of more horror. I cannot repeat the lines: it is in his 'Winter.'" The lines that Gray had in mind were probably these (191-94):

"Then, too, they say, through all the burdened air,
Long groans are heard, shrill sounds and distant sighs
That, uttered by the demon of the night,
Warn the devoted wretch of woe and death."

Thomson appears to have been a sweet-tempered, indolent man, constant in friendship and much loved by his friends. He had a little house and grounds in Kew Lane where he used to compose poetry on autumn nights and loved to listen to the nightingales in Richmond Garden; and where, sang Collins, in his ode on the poet's death (1748),

"Remembrance oft shall haunt the shore,
When Thames in summer wreaths is drest,
And oft suspend the dashing oar
To bid his gentle spirit rest."

Collins had been attracted to Richmond by Thomson's residence there, and forsook the neighborhood after his friend's death.

Joseph Warton, in his "Essay on Pope" (1756), testified that "The Seasons" had been "very instrumental in diffusing a taste for the beauties of nature and landscape." One evidence of this diffused taste was the rise of the new or natural school of landscape gardening. This was a purely English art, and Gray, writing in 1763, says "It is not forty years since the art was born among us; and it is sure that there was nothing in Europe like it": he adds that "our skill in gardening and laying out grounds" is "the only taste we can call our own, the only proof of our original talent in matter of pleasure." "Neither Italy nor France have ever had the least notion of it, nor yet do at all comprehend it, when they see it." Gray's "not forty years" carries us back with sufficient precision to the date of "The Seasons" (1726-30), and it is not perhaps giving undue credit to Thomson, to acknowledge him as, in a great measure, the father of the national school of landscape gardening. That this has always been recognized upon the Continent as an art of English invention, is evidenced by the names Englische Garten, jardin Anglais, still given in Germany and France to pleasure grounds laid out in the natural taste. Schopenhauer gives the philosophy of the opposing styles as follows: "The great distinction between the English and the old French garden rests, in the last analysis, upon this, viz., that the former are laid out in the objective, the latter in the subjective sense, that is to say, in the former the will of Nature, as it manifests (objektivirt) itself in tree, mountain, and water, is brought to the purest possible expression of its ideas, i.e., of its own being. In the French gardens, on the other hand, there is reflected only the will of the owner who has subdued Nature, so that, instead of her own ideas, she wears as tokens of her slavery, the forms which he has forced upon her-clipped hedges, trees cut into all manner of shapes, straight alleys, arched walks, etc."

It would be unfair to hold the false taste of Pope's generation responsible for that formal style of gardening which prevailed when "The Seasons" was written. The old-fashioned Italian or French or Dutch garden—as it was variously called—antedated the Augustan era, which simply inherited it from the seventeenth century. In Bacon's essay on gardens, as well as in the essays on the same subject by Cowley and Sir William Temple, the ideal pleasure ground is very much like that which Le Notre realized so brilliantly at Versailles. Addison, in fact, in the Spectator (No. 414) and Pope himself in the Guardian (No. 173) ridiculed the excesses of the reigning mode, and Pope attacked them again in his description of Timon's Villa in the "Epistle to the Earl of Burlington" (1731), which was thought to be meant for Canons, the seat of the Duke of Chandos.

> "His gardens next your admiration call,
> On every side you look, behold the wall!

No pleasing intricacies intervene,
No artful wildness to perplex the scene;
Grove nods at grove, each alley has a brother,
And half the platform just reflects the other.
The suffering eye inverted nature sees,
Trees cut to statues, statues thick as trees;
With here a fountain, never to be played;
And there a summer house, that knows no shade;
Here Amphitrite sails through myrtle bowers;
There gladiators fight, or die in flowers;
Unwatered see the drooping sea-horse mourn,
And swallows roost in Nilus' dusty urn."

Still the criticism is not merely fanciful which discovers an analogy between the French garden, with its trim regularity and artificial smoothness, and the couplets which Pope wrote: just such an analogy as exists between the whole classical school of poetry and the Italian architecture copied from Palladio and introduced in England by Inigo Jones and Christopher Wren. Grounds were laid out in rectangular plots, bordered by straight alleys, sometimes paved with vari-colored sand, and edged with formal hedges of box and holly. The turf was inlaid with parterres cut in geometric shapes and set, at even distances, with yew trees clipped into cubes, cones, pyramids, spheres, sometimes into figures of giants, birds, animals, and ships—called "topiary work" (opus topiarium). Terraces, fountains, bowling-greens (Fr. boulingrin) statues, arcades, quincunxes, espallers, and artificial mazes or labyrinths loaded the scene. The whole was inclosed by a wall, which shut the garden off from the surrounding country.

"When a Frenchman reads of the Garden of Eden," says Horace Walpole, in his essay "On Modern Gardening" (written in 1770, published in 1785),

"I do not doubt but he concludes it was something approaching to that of Versailles, with clipped hedges, berceaux and trellis work. . . The measured walk, the quincunx and the étoile imposed their unsatisfying sameness on every royal and noble garden. . . Many French groves seem green chests set upon poles. . . In the garden of Marshal de Biron at Paris, consisting of fourteen acres, every walk is buttoned on each side by lines of flower-pots, which succeed in their seasons. When I saw it, there were nine thousand pots of asters, or la reine Marguerite. . . At Lady Orford's, at Piddletown, in Dorsetshire, there was, when my brother married, a double enclosure of thirteen gardens, each I suppose not much above a hundred yards square, with an enfilade of correspondent gates; and before you arrived at these, you passed a narrow gut between two stone terraces that rose above your head, and which were crowned by a line of pyradmidal yews. A bowling green was all the lawn admitted in those times: a circular lake the extent of magnificence."

Walpole names Theobalds and Nonsuch as famous examples of the old formal style of garden; Stourhead, Hagley, and Stowe—the country seat of Lyttelton's brother-in-law, Lord Cobham—of the new. He says that mottoes and coats of arms were sometimes cut in yew, box, and holly. He refers with respect to a recent work by the Rev. Thomas Whately, or Wheatley, "Observations on Modern Gardening," 1770; and to a poem, then and still in manuscript, but passages of which are given by Amherst, entitled "The Rise and Progress of the Present Taste in Planting Parks, Pleasure Grounds, Gardens, etc. In a poetic epistle to Lord Viscount Irwin," 1767.

Gray's friend and editor, the Rev. William Mason, in his poem "The English Garden," 1757, speaks of the French garden as already a thing of the past.

"O how unlike the scene my fancy forms,
Did Folly, heretofore, with Wealth conspire
To plant that formal, dull disjointed scene
Which once was called a garden! Britain still
Bears on her breast full many a hideous wound
Given by the cruel pair, when, borrowing aid
From geometric skill, they vainly strove
By line, by plummet and unfeeling shears
To form with verdure what the builder formed
With stone. . .
Hence the sidelong walls
Of shaven yew; the holly's prickly arms
Trimmed into high arcades; the tonsile box,
Wove in mosaic mode of many a curl
Around the figured carpet of the lawn. . .
The terrace mound uplifted; the long line
Deep delved of flat canal."

But now, continues the poet, Taste "exalts her voice" and

"At the awful sound
The terrace sinks spontaneous; on the green,
Broidered with crispëd knots, the tonsile yews
Wither and fall; the fountain dares no more
To fling its wasted crystal through the sky,
But pours salubrious o'er the parchëd lawn."

The new school had the intolerance of reformers. The ruthless Capability Brown and his myrmidons laid waste many a prim but lovely old garden, with its avenues, terraces, and sun dials, the loss of which is deeply deplored, now that the Queen Anne revival has taught us to relish the rococo beauties which Brown's imitation landscapes displaced.

We may pause for a little upon this "English Garden" of Mason's, as an example of that brood of didactic blank-poems, begotten of Phillips' "Cyder" and Thomson's "Seasons," which includes Mallet's "Excursion" (1728), Somerville's "Chase" (1734), Akenside's "Pleasures of Imagination" (1742-44), Armstrong's "Art of Preserving Health" (1744), Dyer's "Fleece" (1757) and Grainger's "Sugar Cane" (1764). Mason's blank verse, like Mallet's, is closely imitative of Thomson's and the influence of Thomson's inflated diction is here seen at its worst. The whole poem is an object lesson on the absurdity of didactic poetry. Especially harrowing are the author's struggles to be poetic while describing the various kinds of fences designed to keep sheep out of his inclosures.

> "Ingrateful sure,
> When such the theme, becomes the poet's task:
> Yet must he try by modulation meet
> Of varied cadence and selected phrase
> Exact yet free, without inflation bold,
> To dignify that theme."

Accordingly he dignified his theme by speaking of a net as the "sportsman's hempen toils," and of a gun as the

> "—fell tube Whose iron entrails hide the sulphurous blast Satanic engine!"

When he names an ice-house, it is under a form of conundrum:

> "—the structure rude where Winter pounds,
> In conic pit his congelations hoar,
> That Summer may his tepid beverage cool
> With the chill luxury."

This species of verbiage is the earmark of all eighteenth-century poetry and poets; not only of those who used the classic couplet, but equally of the romanticizing group who adopted blank verse. The best of them are not free from it, not even Gray, not even Collins; and it pervades Wordsworth's earliest verses, his "Descriptive Sketches" and "Evening Walk" published in 1793. But perhaps the very worst instance of it is in Dr. Armstrong's "Economy of Love," where the ludicrous contrast between the impropriety of the subject and the solemn pomp of the diction amounts almost to bouffe.

In emulation of "The Seasons" Mason introduced a sentimental love story—Alcander and Nerina—into his third book. He informs his readers (book II. 34-78) that, in the reaction against straight alleys, many gardeners had gone to an extreme in the use of zigzag meanders; and he recommends them to follow the natural curves of the footpaths which the milkmaid wears across the pastures "from stile to stile," or which—"the scudding hare Draws to her dew-sprent seat o'er thymy heaths."

The prose commentary on Mason's poem, by W. Burgh, asserts that the formal style of garden had begun to give way about the commencement of the eighteenth century, though the new fashion had but very lately attained to its perfection. Mason mentions Pope as a champion of the true taste, but the descriptions of his famous villa at Twickenham, with its grotto, thickets, and artificial mounds, hardly suggest to the modern reader a very successful attempt to reproduce nature. To be sure, Pope had only five acres to experiment with, and that parklike scenery which distinguishes the English landscape garden requires a good deal of room. The art is the natural growth of a country where primogeniture has kept large estates in the hands of the nobility and landed gentry, and in which a passion for sport has kept the nobility and gentry in the country a great share of the year. Even Shenstone—whose place is commended by Mason—Shenstone at the Leasowes, with his three hundred acres, felt his little pleasance rather awkwardly dwarfed by the neighborhood of Lyttelton's big park at Hagley.

The general principle of the new or English school was to imitate nature; to let trees keep their own shapes, to substitute winding walks for straight alleys, and natural waterfalls or rapids for jets d'eau in marble basins. The plan upon which Shenstone worked is explained in his "Unconnected Thoughts on Gardening" (1764), a few sentences from which will indicate the direction of the reform: "Landscape should contain variety enough to form a picture upon canvas; and this is no bad test, as I think the landscape painter is the gardener's best designer. The eye requires a sort of balance here; but not so as to encroach upon probable nature.

A wood or hill may balance a house or obelisk; for exactness would be displeasing. . . It is not easy to account for the fondness of former times for straight-lined avenues to their houses; straight-lined walks through their woods; and, in short, every kind of straight line, where the foot has to travel over what the eye has done before. . . To stand still and survey such avenues may afford some slender satisfaction, through the change derived from perspective; but to move on continually and find no change of scene in the least attendant on our change of place, must give actual pain to a person of taste. . . I conceived some idea of the sensation he must feel from walking but a few minutes, immured between Lord D——'s high shorn yew hedges, which run exactly parallel at the distance of about ten feet, and are contrived perfectly to exclude all kind of objects whatsoever. . . The side trees in vistas should be so circumstanced as to afford a probability that they grew by nature. . . The shape of ground, the disposition of trees and the figure of water must be sacred to nature; and no forms must be allowed that make a discovery of art. . . The taste of the citizen and of the mere peasant are in all respects the same: the former gilds his balls, paints his stonework and statues white, plants his trees in lines or circles, cuts his yew-trees, four-square or conic, or gives them what he can of the resemblance of birds or bears or men; squirts up his rivulets in jets d'eau; in short, admires no part of nature but her ductility; exhibits everything that is glaring, that implies expense, or that effects a surprise because it is unnatural. The peasant is his admirer. . . Water should ever appear as an irregular lake or winding stream. . . Hedges, appearing as such, are universally bad. They discover art in nature's province."

It is pertinent to note that there is surely a correspondence between this new taste for picturesque gardening which preferred freedom, variety, irregularity, and naturalness to rule, monotony, uniformity, and artifice, and that new taste in literature which discarded the couplet for blank verse, or for various stanza forms, which left the world of society for the solitudes of nature, and ultimately went, in search of fresh stimulus, to the remains of the Gothic ages and the rude fragments of Norse and Celtic antiquity.

Both Walpole and Mason speak of William Kent, the architect and landscape painter, as influential in introducing a purer taste in the gardener's art. Kent was a friend of Pope and a protégé of Lord Burlington to whom Pope inscribed his "Epistle on the Use of Riches," already quoted and who gave Kent a home at his country house. Kent is said to have acknowledged that he caught his taste in gardening from the descriptive passages in Spenser, whose poems he illustrated. Walpole and Mason also unite in contrasting with the artificial gardening of Milton's time the picture of Eden in "Paradise Lost:"

"—where not nice art in curious knots,
But nature boon poured forth on hill and dale
Flowers worthy of Paradise; while all around
Umbrageous grots, and caves of cool recess,

And murmuring waters, down the slope dispersed,
Or held by fringëd banks in crystal lakes.
Compose a rural seat of various hue."

But it is worth noting that in "L'Allegro" "retired leisure," takes his pleasure in "trim gardens," while in Collins,

"Ease and health retire
To breezy lawn or forest deep."

Walpole says that Kent's "ruling principle was that nature abhors a straight line." Kent "leaped the fence and saw that all nature was a garden. He felt the delicious contrast of hill and valley, changing imperceptibly into each other. . . and remarked how loose groves crowned an easy eminence with happy ornament. . . The great principles on which he worked were perspective and light and shade. . . But of all the beauties he added to the face of this beautiful country, none surpassed his management of water. Adieu to canals, circular basins, and cascades tumbling down marble steps. . . The gentle stream was taught to serpentine seemingly at its pleasure." The treatment of the garden as a part of the landscape in general was commonly accomplished by the removal of walls, hedges, and other inclosures, and the substitution of the ha-ha or sunken fence. It is odd that Walpole, though he speaks of Capability Brown, makes no mention of the Leasowes, whose proprietor, William Shenstone, the author of "The School-mistress," is one of the most interesting of amateur gardeners. "England," says Hugh Miller, "has produced many greater poets than Shenstone, but she never produced a greater landscape gardener."

At Oxford, Shenstone had signalized his natural tastes by wearing his own hair instead of the wig then (1732) universally the fashion. On coming of age, he inherited a Shropshire farm, called the Leasowes, in the parish of Hales Owen and an annuity of some three hundred pounds.

He was of an indolent, retiring, and somewhat melancholy temperament; and, instead of pursuing a professional career, he settled down upon his property and, about the year 1745, began to turn it into a fermé ornée. There he wooed the rustic muse in elegy, ode, and pastoral ballad, sounding upon the vocal reed the beauties of simplicity and the vanity of ambition, and mingling with these strains complaints of Delia's cruelty and of the shortness of his own purse, which hampered him seriously in his gardening designs. Mr. Saintsbury has described Shenstone as a master of "the artificial-natural style of poetry." His pastoral insipidities about pipes and crooks and kids, Damon and Delia, Strephon and Chloe, excited the scorn of Dr. Johnson, who was also at no pains to conceal his contempt for the poet's horticultural pursuits. "Whether to plant a walk in undulating curves and to place a bench at every turn where there is an object to catch the view; to make water run where it will be seen; to leave intervals where the eye will be pleased, and to thicken the plantation where there is something to be hidden, demands any great powers of mind, I will not enquire." The doctor reports that Lyttelton was jealous of the fame which the Leasowes soon acquired, and that when visitors to Hagley asked to see Shenstone's place, their host would adroitly conduct them to inconvenient points of view—introducing them, e.g., at the wrong end of a walk, so as to detect a deception in perspective, "injuries of which Shenstone would heavily complain."

Graves, however, denies that any rivalry was in question between the great domain of Hagley and the poet's little estate. "The truth of the case," he writes, "was that the Lyttelton family went so frequently with their company to the Leasowes, that they were unwilling to break in upon Mr. Shenstone's retirement on every occasion, and therefore often went to the principal points of view, without waiting for anyone to conduct them regularly through the whole walks. Of this Mr. Shenstone would sometimes peevishly complain."

Shenstone describes in his "Thoughts on Gardening," several artifices that he put in practice for increasing the apparent distance of objects, or for lengthening the perspective of an avenue by widening it in the foreground and planting it there with dark-foliaged trees, like yews and firs, "then with trees more and more fady, till they end in the almond-willow or silver osier." To have Lord Lyttelton bring in a party at the small, or willow end of such a walk, and thereby spoil the whole trick, must indeed have been provoking. Johnson asserts that Shenstone's house was ruinous and that "nothing raised his indignation more than to ask if there were any fishes in his water." "In time," continues the doctor, "his expenses brought clamors about him that overpowered the lamb's bleat and the linnet's song; and his groves were haunted by beings very different from fawns and fairies;" to wit, bailiffs; but Graves denies this.

The fame of the Leasowes attracted visitors from all parts of the country—literary men like Spence, Home, and Dodsley; picturesque tourists, who came out of curiosity; and titled persons, who came, or sent their gardeners, to obtain hints for laying out their grounds. Lyttelton brought William Pitt, who was so much interested that he offered to contribute two hundred pounds toward improvements, an offer that Shenstone, however, declined. Pitt had himself some skill in landscape gardening, which he exercised at Enfield Chase and afterward at Hayes. Thomson, who was Lyttelton's guest at Hagley every summer during the last three or four years of his life, was naturally familiar with the Leasowes. There are many references to the "sweet descriptive bard," in Shenstone's poems and a seat was inscribed to his memory in a part of the grounds known as Vergil's Grove. "This seat," says Dodsley, "is placed upon a steep bank on the edge of the valley, from which the eye is here drawn down into the flat below by the light that glimmers in front and by the sound of various cascades, by which the winding stream is agreeably broken. Opposite to this seat the ground rises again in an easy concave to a kind of dripping fountain, where a small rill trickles down a rude niche of rock work through fern, liverwort, and aquatic weeds. . . The whole scene is opaque and gloomy."

English landscape gardening is a noble art. Its principles are sound and of perpetual application. Yet we have advanced so much farther in the passion for nature than the men of Shenstone's day that we are apt to be impatient of the degree of artifice present in even the most skillful counterfeit of the natural landscape. The poet no longer writes odes on "Rural Elegance," nor sings

"The transport, most allied to song,
  In some fair valley's peaceful bound
To catch soft hints from Nature's tongue,
  And bid Arcadia bloom around;
Whether we fringe the sloping hill,
  Or smooth below the verdant mead;
Or in the horrid brambles' room
  Bid careless groups of roses bloom;
Or let some sheltered lake serene
  Reflect flowers, woods and spires, and brighten all the scene."

If we cannot have the mountains, the primeval forest, or the shore of the wild sea, we can at least have Thomson's "great simple country," subdued to man's use but not to his pleasure. The modern mood prefers a lane to a winding avenue, and an old orchard or stony pasture to a lawn decorated with coppices. Howitt says "I do confess," that in the 'Leasowes' I have always found so much ado about nothing; such a parade of miniature cascades, lakes, streams conveyed hither and thither; surprises in the disposition of woods and the turn of walks. . . that I have heartily wished myself out upon a good rough heath."

For the "artificial-natural" was a trait of Shenstone's gardening no less than of his poetry. He closed every vista and emphasized every opening in his shrubberies and every spot that commanded a prospect with come object which was as an exclamation point on the beauty of the scene: a rustic bench, a root-house, a Gothic alcove, a grotto, a hermitage, a memorial urn or obelisk dedicated to Lyttelton, Thomson, Somerville, Dodsley, or some other friend. He supplied these with inscriptions expressive of the sentiments appropriate to the spot, passages from Vergil, or English or Latin verses of his own composition. Walpole says that Kent went so far in his imitation of natural scenery as to plant dead trees in Kensington Garden. Walpole himself seems to approve of such devices as artificial ruins, "a feigned steeple of a distant church or an unreal bridge to disguise the termination of water." Shenstone was not above these little effects: he constructed a "ruinated priory" and a temple of Pan out of rough, unhewn stone; he put up a statue of a piping faun, and another of the Venus dei Medici beside a vase of gold fishes.

Some of Shenstone's inscriptions have escaped the tooth of time. The motto, for instance, cut upon the urn consecrated to the memory of his cousin, Miss Dolman, was prefixed by Byron to his "Elegy upon Thyrza": "Heu quanto minus est cum reliquis versari quam tui meminisse!" The habit of inscription prevailed down to the time of Wordsworth, who composed a number for the grounds of Sir George Beaumont at Coleorton. One of Akenside's best pieces is his "Inscription for a Grotto," which is not unworthy of Landor. Matthew Green, the author of "The Spleen," wrote a poem of some 250 lines upon Queen Caroline's celebrated grotto in Richmond Garden. "A grotto," says Johnson, apropos of that still more celebrated one at Pope's Twickenham villa, "is not often the wish or pleasure of an Englishman, who has more frequent need to solicit than exclude the sun"; but the increasing prominence of the mossy cave and hermit's cell, both in descriptive verse and in gardening, was symptomatic. It was a note of the coming romanticism, and of that pensive, elegiac strain which we shall encounter in the work of Gray, Collins, and the Wartons. It marked the withdrawal of the muse from the world's high places into the cool sequestered vale of life. All through the literature of the mid-century, the high-strung ear may catch the drip-drip of spring water down the rocky walls of the grot.

At Hagley, halfway up the hillside, Miller saw a semi-octagonal temple dedicated to the genius of Thomson. It stood in a grassy hollow which commanded a vast, open prospect and was a favorite resting place of the poet of "The Seasons." In a shady, secluded ravine he found a white pedestal, topped by an urn which Lyttelton had inscribed to the memory of Shenstone. This contrast of situation seemed to the tourist emblematic. Shenstone, he says, was an egotist, and his recess, true to his character, excludes the distant landscape. Gray, who pronounced "The Schoolmistress" a masterpiece in its kind, made a rather slighting mention of its author. "I have read an 8vo volume of Shenstone's letters; poor man! He was always wishing for money, for fame and other distinctions; and his whole philosophy consisted in living, against his will, in retirement and in a place which his taste had adorned, but which he only enjoyed when people of note came to see and commend it." Gray unquestionably profited by a reading of Shenstone's "Elegies," which antedate his own "Elegy Written in a Country Churchyard" (1751).

He adopted Shenstone's stanza, which Shenstone had borrowed from the love elegies of a now forgotten poet, James Hammond, equerry to Prince Frederick and a friend of Cobham, Lyttelton, and Chesterfield. "Why Hammond or other writers," says Johnson, "have thought the quatrain of ten syllables elegiac, it is difficult to tell. The character of the elegy is gentleness and tenuity, but this stanza has been pronounced by Dryden. . .to be the most magnificent of all the measures which our language affords."

It is pertinent to note that next after "The Schoolmistress," the most engaging of Shenstone's poems is his "Pastoral Ballad," written in 1743 in four parts and in a tripping anapestic measure. Familiar to most readers is the stanza beginning:

"I have found out a gift for my fair,
I have found where the wood-pigeons breed."

Dr. Johnson acknowledged the prettiness of the conceit:

"So sweetly she bade me adieu,
I thought that she bade me return;"

and he used to quote and commend the well-known lines "Written at an Inn at Henley:

"Whoe'er has travell'd life's dull round,
Where'er his stages may have been,
May sigh to think he still has found
The warmest welcome at an inn."

As to Shenstone's blank verse—of which there is not much—the doctor says: "His blank verses, those that can read them may probably find to be like the blank verses of his neighbors." Shenstone encouraged Percy to publish his "Reliques." The plans for the grounds at Abbotsford were somewhat influenced by Didsley's description of the Leasowes, which Scott studied with great interest.

In 1744 Mark Akenside, a north country man and educated partly in Scotland, published his "Pleasures of Imagination," afterwards rewritten as "The Pleasures of the Imagination" and spoiled in the process. The title and something of the course of thought in the poem were taken from Addison's series of papers on the subject (Spectator, Nos. 411-421). Akenside was a man of learning and a physician of distinction. His poem, printed when he was only twenty-three, enjoyed a popularity now rather hard to account for. Gray complained of its obscurity and said it was issued nine years too early, but admitted that now and then it rose "even to the best, particularly in description." Akenside was harsh, formal, and dogmatic, as a man. Smollett caricatured him in "Peregrine Pickle." Johnson hated his Whig principles and represents him, when settled at Northampton, as "having deafened the place with clamors for liberty." He furthermore disliked the class of poetry to which Akenside's work belonged, and he told Boswell that he couldn't read it. Still he speaks of him with a certain cautious respect, which seems rather a concession to contemporary opinion than an appreciation of the critic's own. He even acknowledges that Akenside has "few artifices of disgust than most of his brethren of the blank song." Lowell says that the very title of Akenside's poem pointed "away from the level highway of commonplace to mountain paths and less dogmatic prospects. The poem was stiff and unwilling, but in its loins lay the seed of nobler births. Without it, the 'Lines Written at Tintern Abbey' might never have been."

One cannot read "The Pleasures of Imagination" without becoming sensible that the writer was possessed of poetic feeling, and feeling of a kind that we generally agree to call romantic. His doctrine at least, if not his practice, was in harmony with the fresh impulse which was coming into English poetry. Thus he celebrates heaven-born genius and the inspiration of nature, and decries "the critic-verse" and the effort to scale Parnassus "by dull obedience." He invokes the peculiar muse of the new school:

> "*Indulgent* Fancy, *from the fruitful banks*
> Of Avon, whence thy rosy fingers cull
> Fresh flowers and dews to sprinkle on the turf
> Where Shakspeare lies."

But Akenside is too abstract. In place of images, he presents the reader with dissertations. A poem which takes imagination as its subject rather than its method will inevitably remain, not poetry but a lecture on poetry—a theory of beauty, not an example of it. Akenside might have chosen for his motto Milton's lines:

> "How charming is divine philosophy!
> Not harsh and crabbëd, as dull fools suppose,
> But musical as is Apollo's lute."

Yet he might have remembered, too, what Milton said about the duty of poetry to be simple, sensuous, and passionate. Akenside's is nothing of these; it is, on the contrary obscure, metaphysical, and, as a consequence, frigid. Following Addison, he names greatness and novelty, i.e., the sublime and the wonderful, as, equally with beauty, the chief sources of imaginative pleasure, and the whole poem is a plea for what we are now accustomed to call the ideal. In the first book there is a passage which is fine in spirit and—though in a less degree—in expression:

> "Who that from Alpine heights his laboring eye
> Shoots round the wide horizon, to survey
> Nilus or Ganges rolling his bright wave

Through mountains, plains, through empires black with shade.

> And continents of sand, will turn his gaze
> To mark the windings of a scanty rill
> That murmurs at his feet? The high-born soul
> Disdains to rest her heaven-aspiring wing
> Beneath its native quarry. Tired of earth
> And this diurnal scene, she springs aloft
> Through fields of air; pursues the flying storm;
> Rides on the vollied lightning through the heavens;
> Or, yoked with whirlwinds and the northern blast,
> Sweeps the long trace of day."

The hint for this passage was furnished by a paragraph in Addison's second paper (Spectator, 412) and the emotion is the same to which Goethe gives utterance in the well-known lines of "Faust";

> "Doch jedem ist es eingeboren
> Dass sein Gefühl hinauf und vorwärts dringt," etc.

But how greatly superior in sharpness of detail, richness of invention, energy of movement is the German to the English poet!

Akenside ranks among the earlier Spenserians by virtue of his "Virtuoso" (1737) and of several odes composed in a ten-lined variation on Spenser's stanza. A collection of his "Odes" appeared in 1745—the year before Collins' and Joseph Warton's-and a second in 1760. They are of little value, but show here and there traces of Milton's minor poetry and that elegiac sentiment, common to the lyrical verse of the time, noticeable particularly in a passage on the nightingale in Ode XV, book i;, "To the Evening Star." "The Pleasures of Imagination" was the parent of a numerous offspring of similarly entitled pieces, among which are Joseph Warton's "Pleasures of Melancholy," Campbell's "Pleasures of Hope," and Rogers' "Pleasures of Memory."

In the same year with Thomson's "Winter" (1726) there were published in two poetical miscellanies a pair of little descriptive pieces, "Grongar Hill" and "The Country Walk," written by John Dyer, a young Welshman, in the octosyllabic couplet of Milton's "L'Allegro" and "Il Pensoroso."

Dyer was a landscape painter who had been educated at Westminster school, studied under Richardson at London, and spent some time wandering about the mountains of Wales in the practice of his art. "Grongar Hill" is, in fact, a pictorial poem, a sketch of the landscape seen from the top of his favorite summit in South Wales. It is a slight piece of work, careless and even slovenly in execution, but with an ease and lightness of touch that contrast pleasantly with Thomson's and Akenside's ponderosity. When Dyer wrote blank verse he slipped into the Thomsonian diction, "cumbent sheep" and "purple groves pomaceous." But in "Grongar Hill"—although he does call the sun Phoebus—the shorter measure seems to bring shorter words, and he has lines of Wordsworthian simplicity—

> "The woody valleys warm and low,
> The windy summit, wild and high."

or the closing passage, which Wordsworth alludes to in his sonnet on Dyer—"Long as the thrush shall pipe on Grongar Hill":

> "Grass and flowers Quiet treads
> On the meads and mountain heads. . .
> And often, by the murmuring rill,
> Hears the thrush while all is still,
> Within the groves of Grongar Hill."

Wordsworth was attracted by Dyer's love of "mountain turf" and "spacious airy downs" and "naked Snowdon's wide, aerial waste." The "power of hills" was on him. Like Wordsworth, too, he moralized his song. In "Grongar Hill," the ruined tower suggests the transience of human life: the rivers running down to the sea are likened to man's career from birth to death; and Campbell's couplet,

> "'Tis distance lends enchantment to the view
> And robes the mountain in its azure hue,"

is thought to owe something to Dyer's

> "As yon summits soft and fair,
> Clad in colors of the air
> Which to those who journey near
> Barren, brown and rough appear,
> Still we tread the same coarse way,
> The present's still a cloudy day."

Dyer went to Rome to pursue his art studies and, on his return in 1740, published his "Ruins of Rome" in blank verse. He was not very successful as a painter, and finally took orders, married, and settled down as a country parson. In 1757 he published his most ambitious work, "The Fleece," a poem in blank verse and in four books, descriptive of English wool-growing. "The subject of 'The Fleece,' sir," pronounced Johnson, "cannot be made poetical. How can a man write poetically of serges and druggets?" Didactic poetry, in truth, leads too often to ludicrous descents. Such precepts as "beware the rot," "enclose, enclose, ye swains," and

"-the utility of salt Teach thy slow swains";

with prescriptions for the scab, and advice as to divers kinds of wool combs, are fatal. A poem of this class has to be made poetical, by dragging in episodes and digressions which do not inhere in the subject itself but are artificially associated with it. Of such a nature is the loving mention—quoted in Wordsworth's sonnet—of the poet's native Carmarthenshire

"-that soft tract Of Cambria, deep embayed, Dimetian land, By green hills fenced, by Ocean's murmur lulled."

Lowell admired the line about the Siberian exiles, met

"On the dark level of adversity."

Miltonic reminiscences are frequent in Dyer. Sabrina is borrowed from "Comus"; "bosky bourn" and "soothest shepherd" from the same; "the light fantastic toe" from "L'Allegro"; "level brine" and "nor taint-worm shall infect the yearning herds," from "Lycidas"; "audience pure be thy delight, though few," from "Paradise Lost."

7
Representative Writers

It is well accepted fact that every phase of literary history or epoch of a particular literary movement is shaped by the works of different creative writers of particular epoch. It is the entire gamut of literary output of that period after which the movement is named.

As we are concerned here with the romanticism and romantic literature in English, it is necessary to introduce you to notable representative writers of the period. As much is known about personal life, i.e. biography of most of these poets, here we will simply deal with their poetry—style, theme, critical analysis etc. only.

In the galaxy of romantic writer. William Wordworth, S.T. Coleridge, Walter Scott, Lord Byron John Keats, P.B. Shelley, Charles Lamb, Thomas de Quincy, Jane Austen, Walter Landor etc. are the prominent names.

First we will take the pioneers in the field.

I

WILLIAM WORDSWORTH (1770-1850)

It is significant to note that it was in 1797 that tne new romantic movement in our literature assumed definite form. Wordsworth and Coleridge retired to the Quantock Hills, Somerset, and there formed the deliberate purpose to make literature "adapted to interest mankind permanently," which, they declared, classic poetry could never do.

Poetry of Wordsworth

Remarkably, there is often a sense of disappointment when one reads Wordsworth for the first time; and this leads us to speak first of two difficulties which may easily prevent a just appreciation of the poet's worth. The first difficulty is in the reader, who is often puzzled by Wordsworth's absolute simplicity. We are so used to stage effects in poetry, that beauty unadorned is apt to escape our notice.

In fact, Wordsworth set himself to the task of freeing poetry from all its "conceits," of speaking the language of simple truth, and of portraying man and nature as they are; and in this good work we are apt to miss the beauty, the passion, the intensity, that hide themselves under his simplest lines. The second difficulty is in the poet, not in the reader.

It must be confessed that Wordsworth is not always melodious; that he is seldom graceful, and only occasionally inspired. When he is inspired, few poets can be compared with him; at other times the bulk of his verse is so wooden and prosy that we wonder how a poet could have written it. Moreover he is absolutely without humor, and so he often fails to see the small step that separates the sublime from the ridiculous. In no other way can we explain "The Idiot Boy," or pardon the serious absurdity of "Peter Bell" and his grieving jackass.

Lover of Nature

On account of these difficulties it is well to avoid at first the longer works and begin with a good book of selections. When we read these exquisite shorter poems, with their noble lines that live forever in our memory, we realize that Wordsworth is the greatest poet of nature that our literature has produced.

Salient Features of this Poetry

If we go further, and study the poems that impress us, we shall find four remarkable characteristics:

(1) Of all the poets who have written of nature there is none that compares with him in the truthfulness of his representation. Burns, like Gray, is apt to read his own emotions into natural objects, so that there is more of the poet than of nature even in his mouse and mountain daisy; but Wordsworth gives you the bird and the flower, the wind and the tree and the river, just as they are, and is content to let them speak their own message.

(2) Wordsworth is sensitive as a barometer to every subtle change in the world about him. In *The Prelude* he compares himself to an æolian harp, which answers with harmony to every touch of the wind; and the figure is strikingly accurate, as well as interesting, for there is hardly a sight or a sound, from a violet to a mountain and from a bird note to the thunder of the cataract, that is not reflected in some beautiful way in Wordsworth's poetry.

(3) It is the *life* of nature which is everywhere recognized; not mere growth and cell changes, but sentient, personal life; and the recognition of this personality in nature characterizes all the world's great poetry. In his childhood Wordsworth regarded natural objects, the streams, the hills, the flowers, even the winds, as his companions; and with his mature belief that all nature is the reflection of the living God, it was inevitable that his poetry should thrill with the sense of a Spirit that "rolls through all things." Cowper, Burns, Keats, Tennyson,—all these poets give you the outward aspects of nature in varying degrees; but Wordsworth gives you her very life, and the impression of some personal living spirit that meets and accompanies the man who goes

alone through the woods and fields. We shall hardly find, even in the philosophy of Leibnitz, or in the nature myths of our Indians, any such impression of living nature as this poet awakens in us.

(4) No other poet ever found such abundant beauty in the common world. He had not only sight, but insight, that is, he not only sees clearly and describes accurately, but penetrates to the heart of things and always finds some exquisite meaning that is not written on the surface. It is idle to specify or to quote lines on flowers or stars, on snow or vapor. Nothing is ugly or commonplace in his world; on the contrary, there is hardly one natural phenomenon which he has not glorified by pointing out some beauty that was hidden from our eyes.

On Humanity

Such is the philosophy of Wordsworth's nature poetry. If we search now for his philosophy of human life, we shall find four more doctrines, which rest upon his basal conception that man is not apart from nature, but is the very "life of her life."

(1) In childhood man is sensitive as a wind harp to all natural influences; he is an epitome of the gladness and beauty of the world. In his "Intimations of Immortality from Recollections of Early Childhood" (1807), Wordsworth sums up his philosophy of childhood; and he may possibly be indebted here to the poet Vaughan, who, more than a century before, had proclaimed in "The Retreat" the same doctrine. This kinship with nature and with God, which glorifies childhood, ought to extend through a man's whole life and ennoble it. This is the teaching of "Tintern Abbey," in which the best part of our life is shown to be the result of natural influences. According to Wordsworth, society and the crowded unnatural life of cities tend to weaken and pervert humanity; and a return to natural and simple living is the only remedy for human wretchedness.

(2) The *truth* of humanity, that is, the common life which labors and loves and shares the general heritage of smiles and tears, is the only subject of permanent literary interest. Burns and the early poets of the Revival began the good work of showing the romantic interest of common life; and Wordsworth continued it in "Michael," "The Solitary Reaper," "To a Highland Girl," "Stepping Westward," *The Excursion*, and a score of lesser poems. Joy and sorrow, not of princes or heroes, but "in widest commonalty spread," are his themes; and the hidden purpose of many of his poems is to show that the keynote of all life is happiness,—not an occasional thing, the result of chance or circumstance, but a heroic thing, to be won, as one would win any other success, by work and patience.

(3) The natural instincts and pleasures of childhood are the true standards of a man's happiness in this life. All artificial pleasures soon grow tiresome. The natural pleasures, which a man so easily neglects in his work, are the chief means by which we may expect permanent and increasing joy. In "Tintern Abbey," "The Rainbow," "Ode to Duty," and "Intimations of Immortality" we see this plain teaching; but we can hardly read one of Wordsworth's pages without finding it slipped in unobtrusively, like the fragrance of a wild flower.

(4) To this natural philosophy of man Wordsworth adds a mystic element, the result of his own belief that in every natural object there is a reflection of the living God. Nature is everywhere transfused and illumined by Spirit; man also is a reflection of the divine Spirit; and we shall never understand the emotions roused by a flower or a sunset until we learn that nature appeals through the eye of man to his inner spirit. In a word, nature must be "spiritually discerned." In "Tintern Abbey" the spiritual appeal of nature is expressed in almost every line; but the mystic conception of man is seen more clearly in "Intimations of Immortality," which Emerson calls "the high-water mark of poetry in the nineteenth century."

In this last splendid ode Wordsworth adds to his spiritual interpretation of nature and man the alluring doctrine of preëxistence, which has appealed so powerfully to Hindoo and Greek in turn, and which makes of human life a continuous, immortal thing, without end or beginning.

It is worthy to mention that Wordsworth's longer poems, since they contain much that is prosy and uninteresting, may well be left till after we have read the odes, sonnets, and short descriptive poems that have made him famous. As showing a certain heroic cast of Wordsworth's mind, it is interesting to learn that the greater part of his work, including *The Prelude* and *The Excursion*, was intended for a place in a single great poem, to be called *The Recluse*, which should treat of nature, man, and society. *The Prelude*, treating of the growth of a poet's mind, was to introduce the work.

The *Home at Grasmere*, which is the first book of *The Recluse*, was not published till 1888, long after the poet's death. *The Excursion* (1814) is the second book of *The Recluse*; and the third was never completed, though Wordsworth intended to include most of his shorter poems in this third part, and so make an immense personal epic of a poet's life and work. It is perhaps just as well that the work remained unfinished. The best of his work appeared in the *Lyrical Ballads* (1798) and in the sonnets, odes, and lyrics of the next ten years; though "The Duddon Sonnets" (1820), "To a Skylark" (1825), and "Yarrow Revisited" (1831) show that he retained till past sixty much of his youthful enthusiasm.

II

SAMUEL TAYLOR COLERIDGE (1772-1834)

A great companion of William Wordsworth, the works of Coleridge naturally divide themselves into three classes,—the poetic, the critical, and the philosophical, corresponding to the early, the middle, and the later periods of his career.

Of his poetry Stopford Brooke well says: "All that he did excellently might be bound up in twenty pages, but it should be bound in pure gold." His early poems show the influence of Gray and Blake, especially of the latter. When Coleridge begins his "Day Dream" with the line, "My eyes make pictures when they're shut," we recall instantly Blake's haunting *Songs of Innocence*. But there is this difference between the two poets,—in Blake we have only a dreamer; in Coleridge we have the rare combination of the dreamer and the profound scholar.

The quality of this early poetry, with its strong suggestion of Blake, may be seen in such poems as "A Day Dream," "The Devil's Thoughts," "The Suicide's Argument," and "The Wanderings of Cain." His later poems, wherein we see his imagination bridled by thought and study, but still running very freely, may best be appreciated in "Kubla Khan," "Christabel," and "The Rime of the Ancient Mariner." It is difficult to criticise such poems; one can only read them and wonder at their melody, and at the vague suggestions which they conjure up in the mind. "Kubla Khan" is a fragment, painting a gorgeous Oriental dream picture, such as one might see in an October sunset.

"Christabel" is also a fragment, which seems to have been planned as the story of a pure young girl who fell under the spell of a sorcerer, in the shape of the woman Geraldine. It is full of a strange melody, and contains many passages of exquisite poetry; but it trembles with a strange, unknown horror, and so suggests the supernatural terrors of the popular hysterical novels, to which we have referred. On this account it is not wholesome reading; though one flies in the face of Swinburne and of other critics by venturing to suggest such a thing.

"The Rime of the Ancient Mariner" is Coleridge's chief contribution to the *Lyrical Ballads* of 1798, and is one of the world's masterpieces. Though it introduces the reader to a supernatural realm, with a phantom ship, a crew of dead men, the overhanging curse of the albatross, the polar spirit, and the magic breeze, it nevertheless manages to create a sense of absolute reality concerning these manifest absurdities. All the mechanisms of the poem, its meter, rime, and melody are perfect; and some of its descriptions of the lonely sea have never been equaled. Perhaps we should say suggestions, rather than descriptions; for Coleridge never describes things, but makes a suggestion, always brief and always exactly right, and our own imagination instantly supplies the details. It is useless to quote fragments; one must read the entire poem, if he reads nothing else of the romantic school of poetry.

Remarkably, among Coleridge's shorter poems there is a wide variety, and each reader must be left largely to follow his own taste. The beginner will do well to read a few of the early poems, to which we have referred, and then try the "Ode to France," "Youth and Age," "Dejection," "Love Poems," "Fears in Solitude," "Religious Musings," "Work Without Hope," and the glorious "Hymn Before Sunrise in the Vale of Chamouni." One exquisite little poem from the Latin, "The Virgin's Cradle Hymn," and his version of Schiller's *Wallenstein*, show Coleridge's remarkable power as a translator. The latter is one of the best poetical translations in our literature.

Of Coleridge's prose works, the *Biographia, Literaria, or Sketches of My Literary Life and Opinions* (1817), his collected *Lectures on Shakespeare* (1849), and *Aids to Reflection* (1825) are the most interesting from a literary view point. The first is an explanation and criticism of Wordsworth's theory of poetry, and contains more sound sense and illuminating ideas on the general subject of poetry than any other book in our language. The *Lectures*, as refreshing as a west wind in midsummer, are remarkable for their attempt to sweep away the arbitrary rules which for two centuries had stood in the way of literary criticism of Shakespeare, in order to study the works themselves. No finer analysis and appreciation of the master's genius has ever been written. In his philosophical work Coleridge introduced the idealistic philosophy of Germany into England. He set himself in line with Berkeley, and squarely against Bentham, Malthus, Mill, and all the materialistic tendencies which were and still are the bane of English philosophy.

III

WALTER SCOTT (1771-1832)

Of two significant movements of the eighteenth century, the first is the triumph of romantic poetry in Wordsworth and Coleridge; and the second is the success of our first English novelists, and the popularization of literature by taking it from the control of a few patrons and critics and putting it into the hands of the people as one of the forces which mold our modern life. Scott is an epitome of both these movements. The past, which had hitherto appeared as a dreary region of dead heroes, became alive again, and filled with a multitude of men and women who had the surprising charm of reality. It is of small consequence that Scott's poetry and prose are both faulty; that his poems are read chiefly for the story, rather than for their poetic excellence; and that much of the evident crudity and barbarism of the Middle Ages is ignored or forgotten in Scott's writings.

By their vigor, their freshness, their rapid action, and their breezy, out-of-door atmosphere, Scott's novels attracted thousands of readers who else had known nothing of the delights of literature. He is, therefore, the greatest known factor in establishing and in popularizing that romantic element in prose and poetry which has been for a hundred years the chief characteristic of our literature.

Scott's work is of a kind which the critic gladly passes over, leaving each reader to his own joyous and uninstructed opinion. From a literary view point the works are faulty enough, if one is looking for faults; but it is well to remember that they were intended to give delight, and that they rarely fail of their object. When one has read the stirring *Marmion* or the more enduring *Lady of the Lake*, felt the heroism of the Crusaders in *The Talisman*, the picturesqueness of chivalry in *Ivanhoe*, the nobleness of soul of a Scotch peasant girl in *The Heart of Midlothian*, and the quality of Scotch faith in *Old Mortality*, then his own opinion of Scott's genius will be of more value than all the criticisms that have ever been written.

His Poetry

At the outset we must confess frankly that Scott's poetry is not artistic, in the highest sense, and that it lacks the deeply imaginative and suggestive qualities which make a poem the noblest and most enduring work of humanity. We read it now, not for its poetic excellence, but for its absorbing story interest. Even so, it serves an admirable purpose. *Marmion* and *The Lady of the Lake*, which are often the first long poems read by the beginner in literature, almost invariably lead to a deeper interest in the subject; and many readers owe to these poems an introduction to the delights of poetry. They are an excellent beginning, therefore, for young readers, since they are almost certain to hold the attention, and to lead indirectly to an interest in other and better poems. Aside from this, Scott's poetry is marked by vigor and youthful abandon; its interest lies in its vivid pictures, its heroic characters, and especially in its rapid action and succession of adventures, which hold and delight us still, as they held and delighted the first wondering readers. And one finds here and there terse descriptions, or snatches of song and ballad, like the "Boat Song" and "Lochinvar," which are among the best known in our literature.

His Fiction

In his novels Scott plainly wrote too rapidly and too much. While a genius of the first magnitude, the definition of genius as "the infinite capacity for taking pains" hardly belongs to him. For details of life and history, for finely drawn characters, and for tracing the logical consequences of human action, he has usually no inclination. He sketches a character roughly, plunges him into the midst of stirring incidents, and the action of the story carries us on breathlessly to the end. So his stories are largely adventure stories, at the best; and it is this element of adventure and glorious action, rather than the study of character, which makes Scott a perennial favorite of the young. The same element of excitement is what causes mature readers to turn from Scott to better novelists, who have more power to delineate human character, and to create, or discover, a romantic interest in the incidents of everyday life rather than in stirring adventure.

Salient Features

(1) He created the historical novel; and all novelists of the last century who draw upon history for their characters and events are followers of Scott and acknowledge his mastery.

(2) Scott was the first novelist in any language to make the scene an essential element in the action. He knew Scotland, and loved it; and there is hardly an event in any of his Scottish novels in which we do not breathe the very atmosphere of the place, and feel the presence of its moors and mountains. The place, morever, is usually so well chosen and described that the action seems almost to be the result of natural environment. Perhaps the most striking illustration of this harmony between scene and incident is found in *Old Mortality*, where Morton approaches the cave of the old Covenanter, and where the spiritual terror inspired by the fanatic's struggle with imaginary fiends is paralleled by the physical terror of a gulf and a roaring flood spanned by a slippery tree trunk. A second illustration of the same harmony of scene and incident is found in the meeting of the arms and ideals of the East and West, when the two champions fight in the burning desert, and then eat bread together in the cool shade of the oasis, as described in the

opening chapter of *The Talisman.* A third illustration is found in that fascinating love scene, where Ivanhoe lies wounded, raging at his helplessness, while the gentle Rebecca alternately hides and reveals her love as she describes the terrific assault on the castle, which goes on beneath her window. His thoughts are all on the fight; hers on the man she loves; and both are natural, and both are exactly what we expect under the circumstances. These are but striking examples of the fact that, in all his work, Scott tries to preserve perfect harmony between the scene and the action.

(3) His novels are on a vast scale, covering a very wide range of action, and are concerned with public rather than with private interests. So, with the exception of *The Bride of Lammermoor*, the love story in his novels is generally pale and feeble; but the strife and passions of big parties are magnificently portrayed.

A glance over even the titles of his novels shows how the heroic side of history for over six hundred years finds expression in his pages; and all the parties of these six centuries—Crusaders, Covenanters, Cavaliers, Roundheads, Papists, Jews, Gypsies, Rebels—start into life again, and fight or give a reason for the faith that is in them. No other novelist in England, and only Balzac in France, approaches Scott in the scope of his narratives.

(4) Scott's chief claim to greatness lies in the fact that he was the first novelist to recreate the past; that he changed our whole conception of history by making it to be, not a record of dry facts, but a stage on which living men and women played their parts. Carlyle's criticism is here most pertinent: "These historical novels have taught this truth ... unknown to writers of history: that the bygone ages of the world were actually filled by living men, not by protocols, state papers, controversies, and abstractions of men."

Not only the pages of history, but all the hills and vales of his beloved Scotland are filled with living characters,—

lords and ladies, soldiers, pirates, gypsies, preachers, schoolmasters, clansmen, bailiffs, dependents,—all Scotland is here before our eyes, in the reality of life itself. It is astonishing, with his large numbers of characters, that Scott never repeats himself. Naturally he is most at home in Scotland, and with humble people. Scott's own romantic interest in feudalism caused him to make his lords altogether too lordly; his aristocratic maidens are usually bloodless, conventional, exasperating creatures, who talk like books and pose like figures in an old tapestry.

Perhaps one thing more should be said, or rather repeated, of Scott's enduring work. He is always sane, wholesome, manly, inspiring. We know the essential nobility of human life better, and we are better men and women ourselves, because of what he has written.

IV

ROBERT SOUTHEY (1774-1843)

Robert Southey was closely associated with Wordsworth and Coleridge. The three, on account of their residence in the northern lake district, were referred to contemptuously as the "Lakers" by the Scottish magazine reviewers. Southey holds his place in this group more by personal association than by his literary gifts. He was born at Bristol, in 1774; studied at Westminster School, and at Oxford, where he found himself in perpetual conflict with the authorities on account of his independent views. He finally left the university and joined Coleridge in his scheme of a Pantisocracy. For more than fifty years he labored steadily at literature, refusing to consider any other occupation. He considered himself seriously as one of the greatest writers of the day, and a reading of his ballads—which connected him at once with the romantic school—leads us to think that, had he written less, he might possibly have justified his own opinion of himself. Unfortunately he could not wait for inspiration, being obliged to support not only his own family but also, in large measure, that of his friend Coleridge.

Southey gradually surrounded himself with one of the most extensive libraries in England, and set himself to the task of of writing something every working day. The results of his industry were one hundred and nine volumes, besides some hundred and fifty articles for the magazines, most of which are now utterly forgotten. His most ambitious poems are *Thalaba*, a tale of Arabian enchantment; *The Curse of Kehama*, a medley of Hindoo mythology; *Madoc*, a legend of a Welsh prince who discovered the western world; and *Roderick*, a tale of the last of the Goths. All these, and many more, although containing some excellent passages, are on the whole exaggerated and unreal, both in manner and in matter. Southey wrote far better prose than poetry, and his admirable *Life of Nelson* is still often read. Besides these are his *Lives of British Admirals*, his lives of Cowper and Wesley, and his histories of Brazil and of the Peninsular War.

Southey was made Poet Laureate in 1813, and was the first to raise that office from the low estate into which it had fallen since the death of Dryden. The opening lines of Thalaba, beginning,

How beautiful is night!A dewy freshness fills the silent air, are still sometimes quoted; and a few of his best known short poems, like "The Scholar," "Auld Cloots," "The Well of St. Keyne," "The Inchcape Rock," and "Lodore," will repay the curious reader. The beauty of Southey's character, his patience and helpfulness, make him a worthy associate of the two greater poets with whom he is generally named.

V

LORD BYRON (1788-1824)

First it is pertinent to note that are two distinct sides to Byron and his poetry, one good, the other bad; and those who write about him generally describe one side or the other in superlatives. Thus one critic speaks of his "splendid and imperishable excellence of sincerity and strength";

another of his "gaudy charlatanry, blare of brass, and big bow-wowishness." As both critics are fundamentally right, we shall not here attempt to reconcile their differences, which arise from viewing one side of the man's nature and poetry to the exclusion of the other. Before his exile from England, in 1816, the general impression made by Byron is that of a man who leads an irregular life, poses as a romantic hero, makes himself out much worse than he really is, and takes delight in shocking not only the conventions but the ideals of English society.

His poetry of this first period is generally, though not always, shallow and insincere in thought, and declamatory or bombastic in expression. After his exile, and his meeting with Shelley in Italy, we note a gradual improvement, due partly to Shelley's influence and partly to his own mature thought and experience. We have the impression now of a disillusioned man who recognizes his true character, and who, though cynical and pessimistic, is at least honest in his unhappy outlook on society. His poetry of this period is generally less shallow and rhetorical, and though he still parades his feelings in public, he often surprises us by being manly and sincere. Thus in the third canto of *Childe Harold*, written just after his exile, he says:

Notably, in reading Byron it is well to remember that he was a disappointed and embittered man, not only in his personal life, but also in his expectation of a general transformation of human society. As he pours out his own feelings, chiefly, in his poetry, he is the most expressive writer of his age in voicing the discontent of a multitude of Europeans who were disappointed at the failure of the French Revolution to produce an entirely new form of government and society.

Remarkably, one who wishes to understand the whole scope of Byron's genius and poetry will do well to begin with his first work, *Hours of Idleness*, written when he was a young man at the university. There is very little poetry in the volume, only a striking facility in rime, brightened by the devil-may-care spirit of the Cavalier poets; but as a revelation of the man himself it is remarkable. In a vain and sophomoric preface he declares that poetry is to him an idle experiment, and that this is his first and last attempt to amuse himself in that line. Curiously enough, as he starts for Greece on his last, fatal journey, he again ridicules literature, and says that the poet is a "mere babbler." It is this despising of the art which alone makes him famous that occasions our deepest disappointment. Even in his magnificent passages, in a glowing description of nature or of a Hindoo woman's exquisite love, his work is frequently marred by a wretched pun, or by some cheap buffoonery, which ruins our first splendid impression of his poetry.

Byron's later volumes, *Manfred* and *Cain*, the one a curious, and perhaps unconscious, parody of *Faust*, the other of *Paradise Lost*, are his two best known dramatic works. Aside from the question of their poetic value, they are interesting as voicing Byron's excessive individualism and his rebellion against society. The best known and the most readable of Byron's works *Mazeppa, The Prisoner of Chillon*, and *Childe Harold's Pilgrimage*. The first two cantos of *Childe Harold* (1812) are perhaps more frequently read than any other work of the same author, partly because of their melodious verse, partly because of their descriptions of places along the lines of European travel; but the last two cantos (1816-1818) written after his exile from England, have more sincerity, and are in every way better expressions of Byron's mature genius.

Scattered through all his works one finds magnificent descriptions of natural scenery, and exquisite lyrics of love and despair; but they are mixed with such a deal of bombast and rhetoric, together with much that is unwholesome, that the beginner will do well to confine himself to a small volume of well-chosen selections. Byron is often compared with Scott, as having given to us Europe and the Orient, just as Scott gave us Scotland and its people; but while there is a certain resemblance in the swing and dash of the verses, the resemblance is all on the surface, and the underlying difference between the two poets is as great as that between Thackeray and Bulwer-Lytton. Scott knew his country well,—its hills and valleys which are interesting as the abode of living and lovable men and women.

Byron pretended to know the secret, unwholesome side of Europe, which generally hides itself in the dark; but instead of giving us a variety of living men, he never gets away from his own unbalanced and egotistical self. All his characters, in *Cain, Manfred, The Corsair, The Giaour, Childe Harold, Don Juan*, are tiresome repetitions of himself,—a vain, disappointed, cynical man, who finds no good in life or love or anything. Naturally, with such a disposition, he is entirely incapable of portraying a true woman. To nature alone, especially in her magnificent moods, Byron remains faithful; and his portrayal of the night and the storm and the ocean in *Childe Harold* are unsurpassed in our language.

VI

JOHN KEATS (1795-1821)

John Keats was not only the last but also the most perfect of the Romanticists. While Scott was merely telling stories, and Wordsworth reforming poetry or upholding the moral law, and Shelley advocating impossible reforms, and Byron voicing his own egoism and the political discontent of the times, Keats lived apart from men and from all political measures, worshiping beauty like a devotee, perfectly content to write what was in his own heart, or to reflect some splendor of the natural world as he saw or dreamed it to be. He had, moreover, the novel idea that poetry exists for its own sake, and suffers loss by being devoted to philosophy or politics or, indeed, to any cause, however great or small.

"None but the master shall praise us; and none but the master shall blame" might well be written on the fly leaf of every volume of Keats's poetry; for never was there a poet more devoted to his ideal, entirely independent of success or failure. In strong contrast with his contemporary, Byron, who professed to despise the art that made him famous, Keats lived for poetry alone, and, as Lowell pointed out, a virtue went out of him into everything he wrote. In all his work we have the impression of this intense loyalty to his art; we have the impression also of a profound dissatisfaction that the deed falls so far short of the splendid dream.

In this striking sonnet we have a suggestion of Keats's high ideal, and of his sadness because of his own ignorance, when he published his first little volume of poems in 1817. He knew no Greek; yet Greek literature absorbed and fascinated him, as he saw its broken and imperfect reflection in an English translation. Like Shakespeare, who also was but poorly educated in the schools, he had a marvelous faculty of discerning the real spirit of the classics,—a faculty denied to many great scholars, and to most of the "classic" writers of the preceding century,—and so he set himself to the task of reflecting in modern English the spirit of the old Greeks. The imperfect results of this attempt are seen in his next volume, *Endymion*, which is the story of a young shepherd beloved by a moon goddess. The poem begins with the striking lines:

> A thing of beauty is a joy forever;
> Its loveliness increases; it will never
> Pass into nothingness; but still will keep
> A bower quiet for us; and a sleep
>
> Full of sweet dreams, and health, and quiet breathing,

which well illustrate the spirit of Keats's later work, with its perfect finish and melody. It has many quotable lines and passages, and its "Hymn to Pan" should be read in connection with Wordsworth's famous sonnet beginning, "The world is too much with us." The poem gives splendid promise, but as a whole it is rather chaotic, with too much ornament and too little design, like a modern house. That Keats felt this defect strongly is evident from his modest preface, wherein he speaks of *Endymion*, not as a deed accomplished, but only as an unsuccessful attempt to suggest the underlying beauty of Greek mythology.

Keats's third and last volume, *Lamia, Isabella, The Eve of St. Agnes, and Other Poems* (1820), is the one with which the reader should begin his acquaintance with this master of English verse. It has only two subjects, Greek mythology and mediæval romance. "Hyperion" is a magnificent fragment, suggesting the first arch of a cathedral that was never finished. Its theme is the overthrow of the Titans by the young sun-god Apollo. Realizing his own immaturity and lack of knowledge, Keats laid aside this work, and only the pleadings of his publisher induced him to print the fragment with his completed poems. Throughout this last volume, and especially in "Hyperion," the influence of Milton is apparent, while Spenser is more frequently suggested in reading *Endymion*.

Of the longer poems in the volume, "Lamia" is the most suggestive. It is the story of a beautiful enchantress, who turns from a serpent into a glorious woman and fills every human sense with delight, until, as a result of the foolish philosophy of old Apollonius, she vanishes forever from her lover's sight. "The Eve of St. Agnes," the most perfect of Keats's mediæval poems, is not a story after the manner of the metrical romances, but rather a vivid painting of a romantic mood, such as comes to all men, at times, to glorify a workaday world.

It is by his short poems that Keats is known to the majority of present-day readers. Among these exquisite shorter poems we mention only the four odes, "On a Grecian Urn," "To a Nightingale," "To Autumn," and "To Psyche." These are like an invitation to a feast; one who reads them will hardly be satisfied until he knows more of such delightful poetry. Those who study only the "Ode to a Nightingale" may find four things,—a love of account, when he paused in the crowded street tears would spring to his eyes,—tears of pure pleasure at the abundance of so much good life; and when he wrote, he simply interpreted that crowded human life of joy and sorrow, as Wordsworth interpreted the woods and waters, without any desire to change or to reform them.

He has given us the best pictures we possess of Coleridge, Hazlitt, Landor, Hood, Cowden Clarke, and many more of the interesting men and women of his age; and it is due to his insight and sympathy that the life of those far-off days seems almost as real to us as if we ourselves remembered it. Of all our English essayists he is the most lovable; partly because of his delicate, old-fashioned style and humor, but more because of that cheery and heroic struggle against misfortune which shines like a subdued light in all his writings.

VII

PERCY BYSSHE SHELLEY (1792-1822)

There are three classes of men who see visions, and all three are represented in our literature. The first is the mere dreamer, like Blake, who stumbles through a world of reality without noticing it, and is happy in his visions. The second is the seer, the prophet, like Langland, or Wyclif, who sees a vision and quietly goes to work, in ways that men understand, to make the present world a little more like the ideal one which he sees in his vision. The third, who appears in many forms,—as visionary, enthusiast, radical, anarchist, revolutionary, call him what you will,—sees a vision and straightway begins to tear down all human institutions, which have been built up by the slow toil of centuries, simply because they seem to stand in the way of his dream. To the latter class belongs Shelley, a man perpetually at war with the present world, a martyr and exile, simply because of his inability to sympathize with men and society as they are, and because of his own mistaken judgment as to the value and purpose of a vision. As a lyric poet, Shelley is one of the supreme geniuses of our literature; and the reader will do well to begin with the poems which show him at his very best. "The Cloud," "To a Skylark," "Ode to the West Wind," "To Night,"—poems like these must surely set the reader to searching among Shelley's miscellaneous works, to find for himself the things "worthy to be remembered."

Prometheus Unbound (1818-1820), a lyrical drama, is the best work of Shelley's revolutionary enthusiasm, and the most characteristic of all his poems. Shelley's philosophy (if one may dignify a hopeless dream by such a name) was a curious aftergrowth of the French Revolution, namely, that it is only the existing tyranny of State, Church, and society which keeps man from growth into perfect happiness. Naturally Shelley forgot, like many other enthusiasts, that Church and State and social laws were not imposed upon man from without, but were created by himself to minister to his necessities. In Shelley's poem the hero, Prometheus, represents mankind itself,—a just and noble humanity, chained and tortured by Jove, who is here the personification of human institutions. In due time Demogorgon (which is Shelley's name for Necessity) overthrows the tyrant Jove and releases Prometheus (Mankind), who is presently united to Asia, the spirit of love and goodness in nature, while the earth and the moon join in a wedding song, and everything gives promise that they shall live together happy ever afterwards. Shelley here looks forward, not back, to the Golden Age, and is the prophet of science and evolution. If we compare his Titan with similar characters in *Faust* and *Cain*, we shall find this interesting difference,—that while Goethe's Titan is cultured and self-reliant, and Byron's stoic and hopeless, Shelley's hero is patient under torture, seeing help and hope beyond his suffering.

And he marries Love that the earth may be peopled with superior beings who shall substitute brotherly love for the present laws and conventions of society. Such is his philosophy; but the beginner will read this poem, not chiefly for its thought, but for its youthful enthusiasm, for its marvelous imagery, and especially for its ethereal music. Perhaps we should add here that *Prometheus* is, and probably always will be, a poem for the chosen few who can appreciate its peculiar spiritlike beauty. In its purely pagan conception of the world, it suggests, by contrast, Milton's Christian philosophy in *Paradise Regained*.

In reading Shelley's longer poems one must remember that there are in this poet two distinct men: one, the wanderer, seeking ideal beauty and forever unsatisfied; the other, the unbalanced reformer, seeking the overthrow of present institutions and the establishment of universal happiness. *Alastor, or the Spirit of Solitude* (1816) is by far the best expression of Shelley's greater mood. Here we see him wandering restlessly through the vast silences of nature, in search of a loved dream-maiden who shall satisfy his love of beauty. Here Shelley is the poet of the moonrise, and of the tender exquisite fancies that can never be expressed. The charm of the poem lies in its succession of dreamlike pictures; but it gives absolutely no impressions of reality. It was written when Shelley, after his long struggle, had begun to realize that the world was too strong for him. *Alastor* is therefore the poet's confession, not simply of failure, but of undying hope in some better thing that is to come.

Far different in character is *Epipsychidion* (1821), a rhapsody celebrating Platonic love, the most impalpable, and so one of the most characteristic, of all Shelley's works. It was inspired by a beautiful Italian girl, Emilia Viviani, who was put into a cloister against her will, and in whom Shelley imagined he found his long-sought ideal of womanhood. With this should be read *Adonais* (1821), the best known of all Shelley's longer poems. *Adonais* is a wonderful threnody, or a song of grief, over the death of the poet Keats. Even in his grief Shelley still preserves a sense of unreality, and calls in many shadowy allegorical figures,—Sad Spring, Weeping Hours, Glooms, Splendors, Destinies,—all uniting in bewailing the loss of a loved one. The whole poem is a succession of dream pictures, exquisitely beautiful, such as only Shelley could imagine; and it holds its place with Milton's *Lycidas* and Tennyson's *In Memoriam* as one of the three greatest elegies in our language.

Shelley's revolutionary works, *Queen Mab* (1813), *The Revolt of Islam* (1818), *Hellas* (1821), and *The Witch of Atlas* (1820), are to be judged in much the same way as is *Prometheus Unbound*. They are largely invectives against religion, marriage, kingcraft, and priestcraft, most impractical when considered as schemes for reform, but abounding in passages of exquisite beauty, for which alone they are worth reading. In the drama called *The Cenci* (1819), which is founded upon a morbid Italian story, Shelley for the first and only time descends to reality. The heroine, Beatrice, driven to desperation by the monstrous wickedness of her father, kills him and suffers the death penalty in consequence. She is the only one of Shelley's characters who seems to us entirely human.

In his interpretation of nature Shelley suggests Wordsworth, both by resemblance and by contrast. To both poets all natural objects are symbols of truth; both regard nature as permeated by the great spiritual life which animates all things; but while Wordsworth finds a spirit of thought, and so of communion between nature and the soul of man, Shelley finds a spirit of love, which exists chiefly for its own delight; and so "The Cloud," "The Skylark," and "The West Wind," three of the most beautiful poems in our language, have no definite message for humanity. In his "Hymn to Intellectual Beauty" Shelley is most like Wordsworth; but in his "Sensitive Plant," with its fine symbolism and imagery, he is like nobody in the world but himself. Comparison is sometimes an excellent thing; and if we compare Shelley's exquisite "Lament," beginning "O world, O life, O time," with Wordsworth's "Intimations of Immortality," we shall perhaps understand both poets better.

Both poems recall many happy memories of youth; both express a very real mood of a moment; but while the beauty of one merely saddens and disheartens us, the beauty of the other inspires us with something of the poet's own faith and hopefulness. In a word, Wordsworth found and Shelley lost himself in nature.

VIII

LARLES LAMB

The works of Lamb divide themselves naturally into three periods. First, there are his early literary efforts, including the poems signed "C. L." in Coleridge's *Poems on Various Subjects* (1796); his romance *Rosamund Gray* (1798); his poetical drama *John Woodvil* (1802); and various other immature works in prose and poetry. This period comes to an end in 1803, when he gave up his newspaper work, especially the contribution of six jokes, puns, and squibs daily to the *Morning Post* at sixpence apiece. The second period was given largely to literary criticism; and the *Tales from Shakespeare* (1807)—written by Charles and Mary Lamb, the former reproducing the tragedies, and the latter the comedies—may be regarded as his first successful literary venture. The book was written primarily for children; but so thoroughly had brother and sister steeped themselves in the literature of the Elizabethan period that young and old alike were delighted with this new version of Shakespeare's stories, and the *Tales* are still regarded as the best of their kind in our literature. In 1808 appeared his *Specimens of English Dramatic Poets Contemporary with Shakespeare.* This carried out the splendid critical work of Coleridge, and was the most noticeable influence in developing the poetic qualities of Keats, as shown in his last volume.

The third period includes Lamb's criticisms of life, which are gathered together in his *Essays of Elia* (1823), and his *Last Essays of Elia*, which were published ten years later. These famous essays began in 1820 with the appearance of the new *London Magazine*[232] and were continued for many years, such subjects as the "Dissertation on Roast Pig," "Old China," "Praise of Chimney Sweepers," "Imperfect Sympathies," "A Chapter on Ears," "Mrs. Battle's Opinions on Whist," "Mackery End," "Grace Before Meat," "Dream Children," and many others being chosen apparently at random, but all leading to a delightful interpretation of the life of London, as it appeared to a quiet little man who walked unnoticed through its crowded streets. In the first and last essays which we have mentioned, "Dissertation on Roast Pig" and "Dream Children," we have the extremes of Lamb's humor and pathos.

The style of all these essays is gentle, old-fashioned, irresistibly attractive. Lamb was especially fond of old writers and borrowed unconsciously from the style of Burton's *Anatomy of Melancholy* and from Browne's *Religio Medici* and from the early English dramatists. But this style had become a part of Lamb by long reading, and he was apparently unable to express his new thought without using their old quaint expressions. Though these essays are all criticisms or appreciations of the life of his age, they are all intensely personal. In other words, they are an excellent picture of Lamb and of humanity. Without a trace of vanity or self-assertion, Lamb begins with himself, with some purely personal mood or experience, and from this he leads the reader to see life and literature as he saw it. It is this wonderful combination of personal and universal interests, together with Lamb's rare old style and quaint humor, which make the essays remarkable. They continue the best tradition of Addison and Steele, our first great essayists; but their sympathies are broader and deeper, and their humor more delicious than any which preceded them.

IX

THOMAS DE QUINCY (1785-1859)

Like Lamb, de Quincy was a friend and associate of the

Lake poets, making his headquarters in Wordsworth's old cottage at Grasmere for nearly twenty years. Here the resemblance ceases, and a marked contrast begins. As a man, Lamb is the most human and lovable of all our essayists; while De Quincey is the most uncanny and incomprehensible. Lamb's modest works breathe the two essential qualities of sympathy and humor; the greater number of De Quincey's essays, while possessing more or less of both these qualities, are characterized chiefly by their brilliant style. Life, as seen through De Quincey's eyes, is nebulous and chaotic, and there is a suspicion of the fabulous in all that he wrote. Even in *The Revolt of the Tartars* the romantic element is uppermost, and in much of De Quincey's prose the element of unreality is more noticeable than in Shelley's poetry.

It is pertinent to note that De Quincey's works may be divided into two general classes. The first includes his numerous critical articles, and the second his autobiographical sketches. All his works, it must be remembered, were contributed to various magazines, and were hastily collected just before his death. Hence the general impression of chaos which we get from reading them.

From a literary view point the most illuminating of De Quincey's critical works is his. *Literary Reminiscences*. This contains brilliant appreciations of Wordsworth, Coleridge, Lamb, Shelley, Keats, Hazlitt, and Landor, as well as some interesting studies of the literary figures of the age preceding. Among the best of his brilliant critical essays are *On the Knocking at the Gate in Macbeth* (1823), which is admirably suited to show the man's critical genius, and *Murder Considered as One of the Fine Arts* (1827), which reveals his grotesque humor Other suggestive critical works, if one must choose among such a multitude, are his *Letters to a Young Man* (1823), *Joan of Arc* (1847), *The Revolt of the Tartars* (1840), and *The English Mail-Coach* (1849). In the last-named essay the "Dream Fugue" is one of the most imaginative of all his curious works.

Of De Quincey's autobiographical sketches the best known is his *Confessions of an English Opium-Eater* (1821). This is only partly a record of opium dreams, and its chief interest lies in glimpses it gives us of De Quincey's own life and wanderings. This should be followed by *Suspiria de Profundis* (1845), which is chiefly a record of gloomy and terrible dreams produced by opiates. The most interesting parts of his *Suspiria*, showing De Quincey's marvelous insight into dreams, are those in which we are brought face to face with the strange feminine creations "Levana," "Madonna," "Our Lady of Sighs," and "Our Lady of Darkness." A series of nearly thirty articles which he collected in 1853, called *Autobiographic Sketches*, completes the revelation of the author's own life.

Among his miscellaneous works may be mentioned, in order to show his wide range of subjects, *Klosterheim*, a novel, *Logic of Political Economy*, the *Essays on Style and Rhetoric, Philosophy of Herodotus*, and his articles on Goethe, Pope, Schiller, and Shakespeare which he contributed to the *Encyclopedia Britannica*. De Quincey's style is a revelation of the beauty of the English language, and it profoundly influenced Ruskin and other prose writers of the Victorian Age. It has two chief faults,—diffuseness, which continually leads De Quincey away from his object, and triviality, which often makes him halt in the midst of a marvelous paragraph to make some light jest or witticism that has some humor but no mirth in it. Notwithstanding these faults, De Quincey's prose is still among the few supreme examples of style in our language.

Though he was profoundly influenced by the seventeenth-century writers, he attempted definitely to create a new style which should combine the best elements of prose and poetry. In consequence, his prose works are often, like those of Milton, more imaginative and melodious than much of our poetry. He has been well called "the psychologist of style," and as such his works will never be popular; but to the few who can appreciate him he will always be an inspiration to better writing. One has a deeper respect for our English language and literature after reading him.

MISCELLANEOUS WRITERS

One has only to glance back over the authors we have been studying—Wordsworth, Coleridge, Southey, Byron, Shelley, Keats, Scott, Lamb, De Quincey—to realize the great change which swept over the life and literature of England in a single half century, under two influences which we now know as the French Revolution in history and the Romantic Movement in literature. In life men had rebelled against the too strict authority of state and society; in literature they rebelled even more vigorously against the bonds of classicism, which had sternly repressed a writer's ambition to follow his own ideals and to express them in his own way. Naturally such an age of revolution was essentially poetic,—only the Elizabethan Age surpasses it in this respect,—and it produced a large number of minor writers, who followed more or less closely the example of its great leaders. Among novelists we have Jane Austen, Frances Burney, Maria Edgeworth, Jane Porter, and Susan Ferrier,—all women, be it noted; among the poets, Campbell, Moore, Hogg ("the Ettrick Shepherd"), Mrs. Hemans, Heber, Keble, Hood, and "Ingoldsby" (Richard Barham); and among miscellaneous writers, Sidney Smith, "Christopher North" (John Wilson), Chalmers, Lockhart, Leigh Hunt, Hazlitt, Hallam, and Landor. Here is an astonishing variety of writers, and to consider all their claims to remembrance would of itself require a volume. Though these are generally classed as secondary writers, much of their work has claims to popularity, and some of it to permanence. Moore's *Irish Melodies*, Campbell's lyrics, Keble's *Christian Year*, and Jane Porter's *Thaddeus of Warsaw* and *Scottish Chiefs* have still a multitude of readers, where Keats, Lamb, and De Quincey are prized only by the cultured few; and Hallam's historical and critical works are perhaps better known than those of Gibbon, who nevertheless occupies a larger place in our literature. Among all these writers we choose only two, Jane Austen and Walter Savage Landor, whose works indicate a period of transition from the Romantic to the Victorian Age.

Jane Austen (1775-1817)

Like the Lake poets, Jane Austen met with scanty encouragement in her own generation. Her greatest novel, *Pride and Prejudice*, was finished in 1797, a year before the appearance of the famous *Lyrical Ballads* of Wordsworth and Coleridge; but while the latter book was published and found a few appreciative readers, the manuscript of this wonderful novel went begging for sixteen years before it found a publisher. As Wordsworth began with the deliberate purpose of making poetry natural and truthful, so Miss Austen appears to have begun writing with the idea of presenting the life of English country society exactly as it was, in opposition to the romantic extravagance of Mrs. Radcliffe and her school.

But there was this difference,—that Miss Austen had in large measure the saving gift of humor, which Wordsworth sadly lacked. Maria Edgeworth, at the same time, set a sane and excellent example in her tales of Irish life, *The Absentee* and *Castle Rackrent;* and Miss Austen followed up the advantage with at least six works, which have grown steadily in value until we place them gladly in the first rank of our novels of common life. It is not simply for her exquisite charm, therefore, that we admire her, but also for her influence in bringing our novels back to their true place as an expression of human life. It is due partly, at least, to her influence that a multitude of readers were ready to appreciate Mrs. Gaskell's *Cranford*, and the powerful and enduring work of George Eliot.

Very few English writers ever had so narrow a field of work as Jane Austen. Like the French novelists, whose success seems to lie in choosing the tiny field that they know best, her works have an exquisite perfection that is lacking in most of our writers of fiction. With the exception of an occasional visit to the watering place of Bath, her whole life was spent in small country parishes, whose simple country people became the characters of her novels. Her brothers were in the navy, and so naval officers furnish the only exciting elements in her stories; but even these alleged heroes lay aside their imposing martial ways and act like themselves and other people. Such was her literary field, in which the chief duties were of the household, the chief pleasures in country gatherings, and the chief interests in matrimony. Life, with its mighty interests, its passions, ambitions, and tragic struggles, swept by like a great river; while the secluded interests of a country parish went round and round quietly, like an eddy behind a sheltering rock. We can easily understand, therefore, the limitations of Jane Austen; but within her own field she is unequaled. Her characters are absolutely true to life, and all her work has the perfection of a delicate miniature painting. The most widely read of her novels is *Pride and Prejudice;* but three others, *Sense and Sensibility, Emma*, and *Mansfield Park*, have slowly won their way to the front rank of fiction. From a literary view point *Northanger Abbey* is perhaps the best; for in it we find that touch of humor and delicate satire with which this gentle little woman combated the grotesque popular novels of the *Udolpho* type.

Walter Savage Landor (1775-1864)

It is significant to note that while Hazlitt, Lamb, De Quincey, and other romantic critics went back to early English literature for their inspiration, Landor shows a reaction from the prevailing Romanticism by his imitation of the ancient classic writers. His life was an extraordinary one and, like his work, abounded in sharp contrasts. On the one hand, there are his egoism, his unncontrollable anger, his perpetual lawsuits, and the last sad tragedy with his children, which suggests *King Lear* and his daughters; on the other hand there is his steady devotion to the classics and to the cultivation of the deep wisdom of the ancients, which suggests Pindar and Cicero. In his works we find the wild extravagance of *Gebir*, followed by the superb classic style and charm of *Pericles and Aspasia*. Such was Landor, a man of high ideals, perpetually at war with himself and the world.

Landor's reaction from Romanticism is all the more remarkable in view of his early efforts, such as *Gebir*, a wildly romantic poem, which rivals any work of Byron or Shelley in its extravagance. Notwithstanding its occasional beautiful and suggestive lines, the work was not and never has been successful; and the same may be said of all his poetical works. His first collection of poems was published in 1795, his last a full half century later, in 1846. In the latter volume, *The Hellenics*,—which included some translations of his earlier Latin poems, called *Idyllia Heroica,*—one has only to read "The Hamadryad," and compare it with the lyrics of the first volume, in order to realize the astonishing literary vigor of a man who published two volumes, a half century apart, without any appreciable diminution of poetical feeling. In all these poems one is impressed by the striking and original figures of speech which Landor uses to emphasize his meaning.

8

Conclusion

After having a meticulous study of information furnished in the preceding chapters, by now you might have a clear understanding of Romanticism and Romantic literature in English.

In this chapter we wish to furnish the entire information in nutshell to have a quick review. Some pertinent questions which the students of English literature must know and a chronology of events in historical and literary perspectives during the period are also given.

It is pertinent to note that Romantic period extends from the war with the colonies, following the Declaration of Independence, in 1776, to the accession of Victoria in 1837, both limits being very indefinite, as will be seen by a glance at the Chronology following. During the first part of the period especially, England was in a continual turmoil, produced by political and economic agitation at home, and by the long wars that covered two continents and the wide sea between them. The mighty changes resulting from these two causes have given this period the name of the Age of Revolution. The storm center of all the turmoil at home and abroad was the French Revolution, which had a profound influence on the life and literature of all Europe.

On the Continent the overthrow of Napoleon at Waterloo (1815) apparently checked the progress of liberty, which had started with the French Revolution, but in England the case was reversed. The agitation for popular liberty, which at one time threatened a revolution, went steadily forward till it resulted in the final triumph of democracy, in the Reform Bill of 1832, and in a number of exceedingly important reforms, such as the extension of manhood suffrage, the removal of the last unjust restrictions against Catholics, the establishment of a national system of schools, followed by a rapid increase in popular education, and the abolition of slavery in all English colonies (1833). To this we must add the changes produced by the discovery of steam and the invention of machinery, which rapidly changed England from an agricultural to a manufacturing nation, introduced the factory system, and caused this period to be known as the Age of Industrial Revolution.

Remarkably, the literature of the age is largely poetical in form, and almost entirely romantic in spirit. For, as we have noted, the triumph of democracy in government is generally accompanied by the triumph of romanticism in literature. At first the literature, as shown especially in the early work of Wordsworth, Byron, and Shelley, reflected the turmoil of the age and the wild hopes of an ideal democracy occasioned by the French Revolution. Later the extravagant enthusiasm subsided, and English writers produced so much excellent literature that the age is often called the Second Creative period, the first being the Age of Elizabeth. The six chief characteristics of the age are: the prevalence of romantic poetry; the creation of the historical novel by Scott; the first appearance of women novelists, such as Mrs. Anne Radcliffe, Jane Porter, Maria Edgeworth, and Jane Austen; the development of literary criticism, in the work of Lamb, De Quincey, Coleridge, and Hazlitt; the practical and economic bent of philosophy, as shown in the work of Malthus, James Mill, and Adam Smith; and the establishment of great literary magazines, like the *Edinburgh Review*, the *Quarterly*, *Blackwood's*, and the *Athenaeum*.

Now we turn to some questions which a student of English literature must master.

1. What are the general characteristics of the literature of this period? What two opposing tendencies are illustrated in the novels of Scott and Jane Austen? in the poetry of Byron and Wordsworth?

2. Why is this period of Romanticism (1789-1837) called the Age of Revolution? Give some reasons for the influence of the French Revolution on English literature, and illustrate from poems or essays which you have read. Explain the difference between Classicism and Romanticism. Which of these two types of literature do you prefer?

3. *Coleridge*. What are the general characteristics of Coleridge's life? What explains the profound sympathy for humanity that is reflected in his poems? For what, beside his poems, is he remarkable? Can you quote any passages from his poetry which show, the influence of Wordsworth? What are the characters in "The Ancient Mariner"? In what respect is this poem romantic? Give your own reasons for its popularity. Does the thought or the style of this poem impress you? If you have read any of the *Lectures on Shakespeare*, explain why Coleridge's work is called romantic criticism.

4. *Wordsworth*. Tell briefly the story of Wordsworth's life, and name some of his best poems. Why do the *Lyrical Ballads* (1798) mark an important literary epoch? Read carefully, and make an analysis of the "Intimations of Immortality"; of "Tintern Abbey." Can you explain what political conditions are referred to in Wordsworth's "Sonnet on Milton"? in his "French Revolution"? Does he attempt to paint a picture in his sonnet on Westminster Bridge, or has he some other object in view? What is the central teaching of the "Ode to Duty"? Compare Wordsworth's two Skylark poems with Shelley's. Make a brief comparison between Wordsworth's sonnets and those of Shakespeare and of Milton, having in mind the thought, the melody, the view

of nature, and the imagery of the three poets. Quote from Wordsworth's poems to show his belief that nature is conscious; to show the influence of nature on man; to show his interest in children; his sensitiveness to sounds; to illustrate the chastening influence of sorrow. Make a brief comparison between the characters of Wordsworth's "Michael" and of Burns's "The Cotter's Saturday Night." Compare Wordsworth's point of view and method, in the three poems "To a Daisy," with Burns's view, as expressed in his famous lines on the same subject.

5. *Scott*. Tell the story of Scott's life, and name his chief poems and novels. Do you recall any passage from his poetry which suggests his own heroism? Why was he called "the wizard of the North"? What is the general character of his poetry? Compare *Marmion* with one of the old ballads, having in mind the characters, the dramatic interest of the story, and the style of writing. In what sense is he the creator of the historical novel? Upon what does he depend to hold the reader's attention? Compare him, in this respect, with Jane Austen. Which of his characters impress you as being the most lifelike? Name any novels of the present day which copy Scott or show his influence. Read *Ivanhoe* and the *Lady of the Lake*; make a brief analysis of each work, having in mind the style, the plot, the dramatic interest, the use of adventure, and the truth to nature of the different characters.

6. *Byron*. Why is Byron called the revolutionary poet? (Illustrate, if possible, from his poetry.) What is the general character of his work? In what kind of poetry does he excel? (Quote from *Childe Harold* to illustrate your opinion.) Describe the typical Byronic hero. Can you explain his great popularity at first, and his subsequent loss of influence? Why is he still popular on the Continent? Do you find more of thought or of emotion in his poetry? Compare him, in this respect, with Shelley; with Wordsworth. Which is the more brilliant writer, Byron or Wordsworth? Which has the more humor? Which has the healthier mind? Which has

the higher ideal of poetry? Which is the more inspiring and helpful? Is it fair to say that Byron's quality is power, not charm?

7. *Shelley.* What are the chief characteristics of Shelley's poetry? Is it most remarkable for its thought, form, or imagery? What poems show the influence of the French Revolution? What subjects are considered in "Lines written among the Euganean Hills"? What does Shelley try to teach in "The Sensitive Plant"? Compare Shelley's view of nature, as reflected in "The Cloud" or "The West Wind," with Wordsworth's view, as reflected in "The Prelude," "Tintern Abbey," "Daffodils," etc. To what class of poems does "Adonais" belong? What is the subject of the poem? Name others of the same class. How does Shelley describe himself in this poem? Compare Shelley's "Adonais" and Milton's "Lycidas" with regard to the view of life after death as expressed in the poems. What kinds of scenes does Shelley like best to describe? Compare his characters with those of Wordsworth; of Byron. Do you recall any poems in which he writes of ordinary people or of ordinary experiences?

8. *Keats.* What is the essence of Keats's poetical creed, as expressed in the "Ode on a Grecian Urn"? What are the remarkable elements in his life and work? What striking difference do you find between his early poems and those of Shelley and Byron? What are the chief subjects of his verse? What poems show the influence of the classics? of Elizabethan literature? Can you explain why his work has been called literary poetry? Keats and Shelley are generally classed together. What similarities do you find in their poems? Give some reasons why Keats introduces the old Bedesman in "The Eve of Saint Agnes." Name some of the literary friends mentioned in Keats's poetry.

Compare Keats's characters with those of Wordsworth; of Byron. Does Keats ever remind you of Spenser? In what respects? Is your personal preference for Wordsworth, Byron, Shelley, or Keats? Why?

9. *Lamb*. Tell briefly the story of Lamb's life and name his principal works. Why is he called the most human of essayists? His friends called him "the last of the Elizabethans." Why? What is the general character of the *Essays of Elia*? How is the personality of Lamb shown in all these essays? Cite any passages showing Lamb's skill in portraying people. Make a brief comparison between Lamb and Addison, having in mind the subjects treated, the style, the humor, and the interest of both essayists. Which do you prefer, and why?

10. *De Quincey*. What are the general characteristics of De Quincey's essays? Explain why he is called the psychologist of style. What accounts for a certain unreal element in all his work. Read a passage from *The English Mail-Coach*, or from *Joan of Arc*, or from *Levana, Our Lady of Sorrows*, and comment freely upon it, with regard to style, ideas, interest, and the impression of reality or unreality which it leaves.

11. *Landor*. In what respect does Landor show a reaction from Romanticism? What qualities make Landor's poems stand out so clearly in the memory? Why, for instance, do you think Lamb was so haunted by "Rose Aylmer"? Quote from Landor's poems to illustrate his tenderness, his sensitiveness to beauty, his power of awakening emotion, his delicacy of characterization. Do you find the same qualities in his prose? Can you explain why much of his prose seems like a translation from the Greek? Compare a passage from the *Imaginary Conversations* with a passage from Gibbon or Johnson, to show the difference between the classic and the pseudo-classic style. Compare one of Landor's characters, in *Imaginary Conversations*, with the same character in history.

12. *Jane Austen*. How does Jane Austen show a reaction from Romanticism? What important work did she do for the novel? To what kind of fiction was her work opposed? In what does the charm of her novels consist? Make a brief comparison between Jane Austen and Scott (as illustrated

in *Pride and Prejudice* and *Ivanhoe*), having in mind the subject, the characters, the manner of treatment, and the interest of both narratives. Do Jane Austen's characters have to be explained by the author, or do they explain themselves? Which method calls for the greater literary skill? What does Jane Austen say about Mrs. Radcliffe, in *Northanger Abbey*? Does she make any other observations on eighteenth-century novelists?

END OF THE EIGHTEENTH AND BEGINNING OF THE NINETEENTH CENTURY

History

1760-1820.	George III
1789-1799.	French Revolution
1800.	Union of Great Britain and Ireland
1802.	Colonization of Australia
1805.	Battle of Trafalgar
1807.	Abolition of slave trade
1808-1814	Peninsular War
1812.	Second war with United States
1814.	Congress of Vienna
1815.	Battle of Waterloo
1819.	First Atlantic steamship
1820.	George IV (*d.* 1830)
1826.	First Temperance Society
1829.	Catholic Emancipation Bill
1830.	William IV (*d.* 1837) First railway
1832.	Reform Bill
1833.	Emancipation of slaves

1834.	System of national education
1837.	Victoria (*d.* 1901)

Literature

1770-1850.	Wordsworth
1771-1832.	Scott
1796-1816.	Jane Austen's novels
1798.	Lyrical Ballads of Wordsworth and Coleridge
1802.	Scotts Minstrelsy of the Scottish Border
1805-1817.	Scotts poems
1807.	Wordsworth's Intimations of Immortality. Lamb's Tales from Shakespeare
1809-1818.	Byron's Childe Harold
1810-1813.	Coleridge's Lectures on Shakespeare
1814-1831.	Waverley Novels
1816.	Shelley's Alastor
1817.	Coleridge's Biographia Literaria
1817-1820.	Keats's poems
1818-1820.	Shelley's Prometheus
1820.	Wordsworth's Duddon Sonnets
1820-1833.	Lamb's Essays of Elia
1821.	De Quincey's Confessions
1824-1846.	Landor's Imaginary Conversations.
1830.	Tennyson's first poems
1831.	Scott's last novel
1833.	Carlyle's Sartor Resartus Browning's Pauline
1853-1861.	De Quincey's Collected Essays

Appendix

MAJOR EVENTS IN ROMANTIC LITERATURE (1780-1830)

1780

- George Crabbe's *The Candidate*

Births

George Croly; Anna Maria Porter

1781

- George Crabbe's *The Library*

Births

Ebenezer Elliott

Deaths

Richard Jago

1782

- William Cowper's *Poems*

Births

Ann Taylor

1783

Peace of Versailles: England Recognizes USA

- William Blake's *Poetical Sketches*

- Jane Cave's *Poems on Various Subjects*
- George Crabbe's *"The Village*
- *Orlando Furioso*, translated by John Hoole

Births

Reginald Heber; Washington Irving (US); **Jane Taylor**

Deaths

Henry Brooke; John Scott

1784

Births

Leigh Hunt

Deaths

Henry Alline; Bernard Barton; **Samuel Johnson**; Alexander Ross; George Alexander Stevens; **Phillis Wheatley**

1785

- William Cowper's *The Task* in 6 Books
- Thomas Warton made British Poet Laureate

Births

Lady Caroline Lamb; **Thomas Love Peacock**; John Pierpont (US); Samuel Woodworth (US)

Deaths

Richard Glover; Henry Taylor; William Whitehead

1786

- Robert Burns' *Poems, Chiefly in the Scottish Dialect*
- Philp Morin Freneau's *Poems*

Births

Barron Field (Australia); Brian Waller Procter (Barry Cornwall; Brit.)

Deaths

John Collier; Jupiter Hammon (?); Edward Thompson

Floruit

Anne Hecht (Can.)

1787

Births

Richard Henry Dana (US); Margaret Davidson (US); Mary Russell Mitford

Deaths

Moses Browne; Soame Jenyns

1788

- Peter Pindar's *Poetical Works*

Births

R. H. Barham; **George Gordon, Lord Byron**; **Sarah Josepha Hale** (US)

Deaths

William Mickle; Robert Nugent, lord Nugent; Thomas Russell; **Charles Wesley**

1789

GEORGE WASHINGTON BECOMES PRESIDENT OF USA

- William Blake's *Songs of Innocence* and ***"The Book of Thel***

- Erasmus Darwin's *The Loves of the Plants*, republished in 1791 as *The Botanic Garden*, part II

Births

Charlotte Elliott; **William Knox** (Scotland); **Thomas Pringle** (South Africa); Richard Henry Wilde (US)

Deaths

Frances Brooke; Frances Greville

1790

- William Blake's *The Marriage of Heaven and Hell*
- Henry James Pye made British Poet Laureate
- Literary Fund Society established by David Williams (by 1818 the Royal Literary Fund) to aid indigent authors

Births

Fitz-Greene Halleck (US)

Deaths

Andrew Macdonald; **Thomas Warton** the younger

1791

- Anna Laetitia Barbauld's *Eighteen Hundred and Eleven*
- William Blake's ***"The French Revolution***
- Robert Burns' ***"Tam o'Shanter***
- Erasmus Darwin's *The Botanic Garden*, part I ("The Economy of Vegetation")
- ***Mother Goose's Melodies*** (originally published about 1781)

Births

John Howard Payne (US); Lydia Howard Sigourney (US); **Charles Wolfe** (Ireland)

Deaths

John Frederick Bryant; John Ellis; **Francis Grose**; **John Wesley**; William Woty

1792

- William Blake's *Song of Liberty*
- Samuel Rogers' *The Pleasures of Memory*

Births

John Frederick William Herschel; **Percy Bysshe Shelley**

1793

- William Blake's *Visions of the Daughters of Albion* and *America, A Prophecy*
- Robert Burns' *Poems*
- William Wordsworth's *An Evening Walk* and *Descriptive Sketches*

Births

John Clare; **Felicia Dorothea Hemans**; **Henry Francis Lyte**; John Neal (US); Standish O'Grady (Canada) about this year

Deaths

Gilbert White

1794

- William Blake's *Songs of Experience*, *Europe, A Prophecy*, and ***"The Book of Urizen***

Births

Maria Gowen Brooks (?); William Cullen Bryant (US); Carlos Wilcox (US)

Deaths

Susanna Blamire; Alison Cockburn

1795

- William Blake's *The Book of Los*, *The Book of Ahania*, *The Song of Los*, and *The Songs of Innocence and Experience*
- Philip Morin Freneau's *Poems*
- Walter Savage Landor's *Poems*
- *Robin Hood: A Collection of all the Ancient Poems*, edited by Joseph Ritson

Births

Thomas Carlyle; George Darley; Joseph Rodman Drake (US); **John Keats**; James Gates Percival; Janet Thomson (Scotland)

Deaths

Samuel Bishop

1796

- Joel Barlow's *The Hasty Pudding*
- S. T. Coleridge's *Poems on Various Subjects*

Births

John Gardiner Calkins Brainard (US); **Hartley Coleridge**; Eliza Dunlop (Australia); John Hamilton Reynolds

Deaths

Robert Burns, from rheumatic heart disease; Thomas Cole; John Maclaurin, lord Dreghorn; **James Macpherson**

1797

- William Blake illustrates Edward Young's *Night Thoughts*

- S. T. Coleridge composes **"Kubla Khan"** in an opium-induced dream and writes down only a fragment of it on waking.
- Robert Southey's *Poems*

Births

Thomas Haynes Bayley; **George Moses Horton** (US), about this time; William Motherwell (Scotland)

Deaths

John Codrington Bampfylde; George Keate; William Mason

1798

- G. Canning and J. H. Frere parody Erasmus Darwin's *The Loves of the Plants* in their "The Loves of the Triangles"
- first edition of ***Lyrical Ballads*** by William Wordsworth and Samuel Taylor Coleridge (with Coleridge's ***Rime of the Ancient Mariner***), revised in 1800 and 1802

Births

Macdonald Clarke (US); Samuel Henry Dickson (US); David Macbeth Moir (Scotland)

Deaths

Mary Alcock; Edmund Gardner; Robert Merry

1799

- T. Campbell's ***"The Pleasures of Hope***

Births

A. Bronson Alcott (US); **Thomas Hood**; **Mary Howitt**

Present-day English 1800-present

1800

- The life and works of Robert Burns published

Births

Caroline Clive; **Thomas Babington Macaulay**

Deaths

William Cowper; **Mary Robinson**; **Joseph Warton**

1801

THOMAS JEFFERSON, PRESIDENT OF USA

- Thomas Moore's *Poems by Thomas Little*
- Robert Southey's *Thalaba the Destroyer*

Births

William Barnes; Thomas Cole (US); **John Henry Newman**

Deaths

James Hurdis

1802

- *Ancient English Metrical Romances*, edited by Joseph Ritson
- S. T. Coleridge's **"Dejection: An Ode"**
- Walter Savage Landor's *Poetry by the Author of Gebir*
- Amelia Opie's *Poems*
- Sir Walter Scott's *Minstrelsy of the Scottish Border* (1802-03), an anthology of ballads

Births

Lydia Maria Child (US); Sara Coleridge (daughter of S.T.C.); **Letitia Elizabeth Landon**

("L.E.L."); George Pope Morris (US); Edward Coote Pinkney (US); **Winthrop Mackworth Praed**; Isaac Williams

Deaths

Erasmus Darwin

1803

Births

Thomas Lovell Beddoes; **Ralph Waldo Emerson** (US); **Robert Stephen Hawker**; James Clarence Mangan (Ireland); **Susanna Moodie** (Canada); Sarah Helen Whitman (US)

Deaths

James Beattie; Joseph Ritson

1804

- William Blake's "***Jerusalem***, completed in 1820, and his "***Milton***, completed in 1808
- Ann and Jane Taylor's *Original Poems for Infant Minds*
- William Wordsworth's "Daffodils"

Births

Nathaniel Hawthorne (US); **Joseph Howe** (Canada); Francis Sylvester Mahony, aka Father Prout; Charles Whitehead

Deaths

Joseph Fawcett; Richard Graves; Joseph Mather

1805

- H. F. Cary's translation of Dante's *Inferno*
- *The Comic Adventures of Old Mother Hubbard and her Dog*

- Sir Roger Newdigate founds the Newdigate Prize for English Poetry at Oxford
- Sir Walter Scott's ***"The Lay of the Last Minstrel***
- Robert Southey's *Madoc*
- William Wordsworth finishes a first version of ***"The Prelude: or, Growth of a Poet's Mind*** in 13 Books

Births

Sarah Fuller Flower, née Adams (Representative Poetry Online)

Deaths

Christopher Anstey; Sophia Burrell

1806

- Lord Byron's *Fugitive Pieces*
- William Roscoe's ***The Butterfly's Ball and the Grasshopper's Feast***, a children's classic
- Walter Savage Landor's *Simonidea*
- Thomas Moore's *Epistles, Odes, and Other Poems*
- Sir Walter Scott's *Ballads and Lyrical Pieces*
- Jane and Ann Taylor's *Rhymes for the Nursery*, including **"Twinkle, twinkle, little star"**

Births

Elizabeth Barrett, later Browning; William Gilmore Simms (US); Nathaniel Parker Willis (US)

Deaths

Thomas Morris (?); **Charlotte Smith**; Ann Yearsley

1807

- Joel Barlow's *The Columbiad*

- Lord Byron's *Hours of Idleness* and *Poems on Various Occasions*
- George Crabbe's *Poems* and "The Parish Register"
- Thomas Moore's *Irish Melodies*
- William Wordsworth's *Poems in Two Volumes*, including "Intimations of Immortality"

Births

Henry Louis Vivian Derozio (India); Henry Wadsworth Longfellow; John Greenleaf Whittier (US)

Deaths

John Carr; John Newton

1808

- Sir Walter Scott's ***"Marmion, A Tale of Flodden Field***

Births

Lucretia Maria Davidson; **Evan MacColl** (Canada)

Deaths

Isaac Bickerstaffe (?); John Freeth; Thomas Moss

1809

- Lord Byron's ***"English Bards and Scotch Reviewers***; Byron spent the next two years abroad, notably in Greece
- T. Campbell's *Gertrude of Wyoming* .
- Samuel Taylor Coleridge's *The Friend* 1809-10
- Charles and Mary Lamb's *Poetry for Children*

Births

John Barr (New Zealand); **David Bates** (US);

Thomas Holley Chivers (US); **Edward Fitzgerald**; **Kasiprasad Ghose** (India); **Oliver Wendell Holmes** (US); Fanny Kemble (US); **Abraham Lincoln** (US); Monckton Milnes; **Edgar Allan Poe** (US); **Alfred Tennyson**

Deaths

Mrs. Hannah Cowley; Thomas Holcroft; Anna Seward

1810

- William Blake's engravings for Chaucer's *Canterbury Tales*
- *Gammer Gurton's Garland or the Nursery Parnassus*, including "Little Bo-peep has lost her sheep"
- George Crabbe's *The Borough* in 24 epistles, including one on "**Peter Grimes**, a poem based on Aldeburgh
- Sir Walter Scott's "***The Lady of the Lake***
- Percy Bysshe Shelley's *Original Poetry by Victor and Cazire* and *Zastrozzi*

Births

Margaret Fuller (US); **William Miller** (Scotland); **Edmund Hamilton Sears** (US); Martin Farquhar Tupper

1811

- Sir Walter Scott's *The Vision of Don Roderick*
- Oxford University expells Percy Bysshe Shelley

Births

Arthur Hallam; **William Makepeace Thackeray**

Deaths

John Leyden; **Thomas Percy**

1812

- Lord Byron's *Childe Harold*, Parts I-II, and *The Curse of Minerva*
- H. F. Cary's translation of Dante's *Purgatorio* and *Paradiso*
- Robert Southey's and Samuel Taylor Coleridge's *Omniana* (prose)

Births

Robert Browning; Charles Dickens; Edward Lear

Deaths

Joel Barlow

1813

- Lord Byron's *The Bride of Abydos* and *The Giaour*
- Samuel Taylor Coleridge's *Remorse*
- Sir Walter Scott's "***Rokeby*** and *The Bride of Triermain*
- Percy Bysshe Shelley's "***Queen Mab***
- Robert Southey made British Poet Laureate

Births

William Edmondstone Aytoun (Scotland); Charles Timothy Brooks (US); Christopher Pearse Cranch (US); Epes Sargent (US); Jones Very (US)

Deaths

Henrietta Battier; Jane Cave; Henry James Pye

1814

- Lord Byron's *The Corsair*, "***Lara***, and *Ode to Napoleon*
- Augusta Gordon bore her half-brother Lord Byron's daughter

- Francis Scott Key on Sept. 14 writes **"The Star-Spangled Banner"** during the British attack on Baltimore, Maryland
- Robert Southey's *Roderick, the Last of the Goths*
- William Wordsworth's *The Excursion*

Births

Sarah Tittle Bolton, née Barrett; **James Joseph Sylvester**; Aubrey Thomas De Vere

Deaths

Charles Dibdin; Samuel Jackson Pratt; Edward Rushton

1815

- Lord Byron's *Hebrew Melodies*, including **"The Destruction of Sennacherib"**
- marriage of Lord Byron to Annabella Milbanke
- Philip Morin Freneau's *Poems*
- Leigh Hunt was jailed (1815-17) for criticizing the Prince Regent in *The Examiner*
- Sir Walter Scott's *The Lord of the Isles*
- William Wordsworth's *Poems*

Births

Daniel Decatur Emmett (US)

Deaths

George Ellis; Samuel Henley

1816

- Lord Byron's *The Prisoner of Chillon and other Poems*, "**Childe Harold**, Part III, and *The Siege of Corinth*; he leaves England permanently for Geneva
- Samuel Taylor Coleridge's *Christabel and Other Poems*, including **"Kubla Khan"**

- Leigh Hunt publishes an essay on Percy Bysshe Shelley and John Keats in *The Examiner*, and *The Story of Rimini*
- John Keats is certified as an apothecary and publishes **"On First Looking into Chapman's Homer"**
- Percy Bysshe Shelley marries Mary Woolstonecraft Godwin
- Percy Bysshe Shelley's *Alastor and Other Poems*
- Robert Southey's *A Poet's Pilgrimage to Waterloo*

Births

Philip James Bailey; **Charlotte Brontë**; **Shirley Brooks** (Representative Poetry Online); Frances Brown (Browne); Josiah D. Canning (US); Philip Pendleton Cooke (US); Charles Heavysege (Canada)

Deaths

Richard Brinsley Sheridan

1817

- Lord Byron's "***Manfred*** and *The Lament of Tasso*
- S. T. Coleridge's ***Biographia Literaria***, Vol. I
- John Keats' *Poems*
- John Gibson Lockhart in the October *Blackwood's Magazine* vilifies the "Cockney School of Poetry," said to include Leigh Hunt, William Hazlitt, John Keats and others
- Thomas Moore's "***Lalla Rookh***
- Sir Walter Scott's *Harold the Dauntless*
- Percy Bysshe Shelley's *Laon and Cythna*

Births

Cornelius Mathews (US); **Henry David Thoreau**

(Academy of American Poets Web site; US); John McPherson (Canada)

Deaths

Ann Batten Cristall (this year or after)

1818

- Lord Byron's "***Childe Harold's Pilgrimage***, Book IV, and *Beppo*
- John Wilson Croker's anonymous review attacks John Keats' *Endymion* in the *Quarterly Review*
- William Hazlitt's *Lectures on the English Poets*
- Leigh Hunt's *Foliage*
- John Keats' "***Endymion*** published; he falls in love with Fanny Brawne (1800-65) and writes his great odes this year and the next
- Thomas Love Peacock's *Rhododaphne*
- Percy Bysshe Shelley's *The Revolt of Islam*, originally *Laon and Cythna* (1817); he leaves England.

Births

Cecil Frances Alexander, née Humphreys; **Emily Brontë**; William Ellery Channing (US); **Eliza Cook**; Alexander McLachlan (Canada); John Mason Neale

Deaths

Matthew Gregory Lewis; John Williams

1819

- Lord Byron's *Mazeppa* and "***Don Juan***, I and II
- John Keats falls sick and his writing ceases after **"To Autumn"** in September
- Percy Bysshe Shelley's *The Cenci* and *Rosalind and Helen*; he writes **"Ode to the West Wind"** on

October 1819 in a wood by the Arno River near Florence

- William Wordsworth's *Peter Bell* and *The Waggoner*

Births

A. H. Clough; Thomas Dunn English (US); **Mary Ann Evans** (pseud. "George Eliot"); Josiah Gilbert Holland (US); **Julia Ward Howe** (US); **Charles Kingsley**; James Russell Lowell (US); **Herman Melville** (US); William Wetmore Story (US); **Walt Whitman** (US)

Deaths

John Wolcot

1820

GEORGE III (-1830)

- Elizabeth Barrett's *The Battle of Marathon*
- John Clare's *Poems, Descriptive of Rural Life and Scenery*
- Introduction of the limerick in *The History of Sixteen Wonderful Old Women*
- John Keats' *Lamia, The Eve of St. Agnes, Hyperion, and Other Poems*
- Thomas Love Peacock's ***The Four Ages of Poetry***, which sparked Shelley to write his ***Defence of Poetry***
- Percy Bysshe Shelley's *Prometheus Unbound and Other Poems*, and his essay on a philosophical view of reform (published in 1920)
- William Wordsworth's *The River Duddon* and *Vaudracour and Julia*
- formation of the Apostles, a Cambridge intellectual society

Births

Anne Brontë; Henry Howard Brownell (US); Alice Patty Lee Cary (US); John Harris (Cornwall); John Henry Hopkins, Jr. (US); Jean Ingelow; **William J. Macquorn Rankine** (Scotland)

Deaths

Joseph Rodman Drake; William Hayley; James Woodhouse

1821

- William Cullen Bryant's *Poems*
- John Clare's *The Village Minstrel*
- John Hamilton Reynolds' *The Garden of Florence*
- Percy Bysshe Shelley publishes ***Epipsychidion*** and ***Adonais*** (on John Keats) and writes his *Defence of Poetry*
- Robert Southey's *A Vision of Judgement*

Births

Charles Baudelaire (France); (Academy of American Poets Web site; US) Isabella Banks, née Varley; **Frederick Locker Lampson**; Maria White Lowell (US); Frederick Goddard Tuckerman (US)

Deaths

Anne Hunter; **John Keats** (Feb., in Rome), of tuberculosis

1822

- Lord Byron's *Werner* and his review of Robert Southey's "The Vision of Judgement" in *The Liberal*
- Percy Bysshe Shelley's "***Hellas***

Births

Matthew Arnold; Thomas Buchanan Read (US); Charles Sangster (Canada); James Monroe Whitfield (US)

Deaths

John Aikin; **Percy Bysshe Shelley**, in August, by drowning

1823

- Lord Byron's "***Don Juan***, VI-XIV, and ***Vision of Judgement***
- **"An Account of a Visit from St. Nicholas"** (attributed Major Henry Livingston, Jr.)
- John H. Payne's **"Home Sweet Home"** written, the theme song of Sir Henry Rowley Bishop's opera *Clari*

Births

George Henry Boker (US); **William Johnson Cory**; Margaret Miller Davidson (US); James Mathewes Legaré; Coventry Patmore; William Brighty Rands; Anna Letitia Waring;

Deaths

William Combe; Charles Wolfe

1824

- Lord Byron's *Don Juan*, XV-XVI, and *The Deformed Transformed*,
- Percy Bysshe Shelley's **"The Triumph of Life"**

Births

William Allingham (Ireland); **Sabine Baring-Gould**; **Phoebe Cary** (US); **Sydney Thompson Dobell**; Charles Godfrey Leland (US); George MacDonald (Scotland); George Boyer Vashon (US)

Deaths

Lord Byron, by fever in Greece; Elizabeth Cobbold; Thomas Maurice

1825

Births

Peter John Allan (Canada); **John Askham**; **Henrietta Anne Huxley**; **Thomas Henry Huxley**; **Adelaide Anne Procter**; Bayard Taylor (US); **Frances Ellen Watkins** (US)

Deaths

Lady Anne Barnard; **Anna Laetitia Barbauld**; Mary Darwall; Lucretia Maria Davidson; **William Knox** (Scotland); Lady Anne Lindsay

1826

- Elizabeth Barrett (Browning)'s *An Essay on Mind and Other Poems*

Births

Dinah Maria Mulock Craik; **Stephen Foster** (US); **Robert Lowry** (US)

Deaths

Reginald Heber; John Taylor

1827

- John Clare's *The Shepherd's Calendar*
- Edgar Allan Poe's *Tamerlane and Other Poems*

Births

Rose Terry Cooke (US); Francis Miles Finch (US); **James McIntyre**, poet of the mammoth cheese (Canada); John Hollin Ridge (US); John Townsend Trowbridge (US); **Septimus Winner**

(Representative Poetry Online)

Deaths

William Blake; **George Canning**; Carlos Wilcox

1828

- Felicia Hemans' *Records of Women, with Other Poems*
- John Gibson Lockhart's *Life of Robert Burns*

Births

George Meredith; Arthur Joseph Munby; **Dante Gabriel Rossetti**; Henry Timrod (US)

Deaths

John Gardiner Calkins Brainard; Lady Caroline Lamb; Edward Coote Pinkney

1829

- Thomas Hood's *The Dream of Eugene Aram*
- Edgar Allan Poe's *Al Aaraaf, Tamerlane, and Other Poems*
- Samuel Kettell's *Specimens of American Poetry*

Births

Rosanna Eleanor (Mullins) Leprohon (Canada); **Elizabeth Siddall**;

Deaths

William Crowe; Sir Humphry Davy

1830

WILLIAM IV (-1837)

- Ebenezer Elliott's *Corn Law Rhymes*
- Sarah Josepha Hale's *Poems for our Children*, including **"Mary's Lamb"**
- Alfred Tennyson's *Poems, Chiefly Lyrical*, including "The Kraken"

Births

Charlotte Alington Barnard; **Thomas Edward Brown**; **Emily Dickinson** (US); Paul Hamilton Hayne (US); **Helen Hunt Jackson** (US); **William McGonagall** (ca; Scotland); **Christina Rossetti**; Alexander Smith (?); James M. Whitfield (US)

Deaths

William Hazlitt

1831

- Walter Savage Landor's *Gebir, Count Julian*
- Edgar Allan Poe's *Poems*

Births

Charles Stuart Calverley; **Isa Craig** (Scotland); Edward Robert Bulwer Lytton; **James Clerk Maxwell**; **David Mills** (Canada)

Deaths

Henry Louis Vivian Derozio (India); Laurence Hynes Halloran; **William Roscoe**

1832

- Alfred Tennyson's *Poems* (dated 1833), including **"The Lady of Shalott"** and **"The Lotos-Eaters"**

Births

Elizabeth Akers Allen (US); Sir Edwin Arnold; Benjamin Paul Blood (US); **Lewis Carroll (Charles Lutwidge Dodgson)**; **Joseph Skipsey**; **Henry Clay Work** (US)

Deaths

James Bisset; **George Crabbe**; Philip Morin Freneau; James Plumptre; Anna Maria Porter; **Sir Walter Scott**

Glossary

Alexandrine: A line of poetry that has 12 syllables. The name probably comes from a medieval romance about Alexander the Great that was written in 12-syllable lines.

Alliteration: The repetition of the same or similar sounds at the beginning of words: "What would the world be, once bereft/Of wet and wildness?" (Gerard Manley Hopkins, "Inversnaid")

Anapest: A metrical foot of three syllables, two short (or unstressed) followed by one long (or stressed), as in *seventeen* and *to the moon.* The anapest is the reverse of the dactyl.

Antithesis: A figure of speech in which words and phrases with opposite meanings are balanced against each other. An example of antithesis is "To err is human, to forgive, divine." (Alexander Pope)

Apostrophe: Words that are spoken to a person who is absent or imaginary, or to an object or abstract idea. The poem God's World by Edna St. Vincent Millay begins with an apostrophe: "O World, I cannot hold thee close enough!/Thy winds, thy wide grey skies!/ Thy mists that roll and rise!"

Assonance: The repetition or a pattern of similar sounds, especially vowel sounds: "Thou still unravished bride of quietness,/Thou foster child of silence and slow time" ("Ode to a Grecian Urn," John Keats).

Ballade: A type of poem, usually with three stanzas of seven, eight, or ten lines and a shorter final stanza (or envoy) of four or five lines. All stanzas end with the same one-line refrain.

Blank verse: Poetry that is written in unrhymed iambic pentameter. Shakespeare wrote most of his plays in blank verse.

Caesura: A natural pause or break in a line of poetry, usually near the middle of the line. There is a caesura right after the question mark in the first line of this sonnet by Elizabeth Barrett Browning: "How do I love thee? Let me count the ways."

Canzone: A medieval Italian lyric poem, with five or six stanzas and a shorter concluding stanza (or envoy). The poets Petrarch and Dante Alighieri were masters of the canzone.

Carpe diem: A Latin expression that means "seize the day." Carpe diem poems urge the reader (or the person to whom they are addressed) to live for today and enjoy the pleasures of the moment. A famous carpe diem poem by Robert Herrick begins "Gather ye rosebuds while ye may..."

Chanson de geste: An epic poem of the 11th to the 14th century, written in Old French, which details the exploits of a historical or legendary figure, especially Charlemagne.

Classicism: The principles and ideals of beauty that are characteristic of Greek and Roman art, architecture, and literature. Examples of classicism in poetry can be found in the works of John Dryden and Alexander Pope, which are characterized by their formality, simplicity, and emotional restraint.

Conceit: A fanciful poetic image or metaphor that likens one thing to something else that is seemingly very different. An example of a conceit can be found in Shakespeare's sonnet "Shall I compare thee to a summer's day?" and in Emily Dickinson's poem "There is no frigate like a book."

Consonance: The repetition of similar consonant sounds, especially at the ends of words, as in *lost* and *past* or *confess* and *dismiss*.

Couplet: In a poem, a pair of lines that are the same length and usually rhyme and form a complete thought. Shakespearean sonnets usually end in a couplet.

Dactyl: A metrical foot of three syllables, one long (or stressed) followed by two short (or unstressed), as in *happily*. The dactyl is the reverse of the anapest.

Elegy: A poem that laments the death of a person, or one that is simply sad and thoughtful. An example of this type of poem is Thomas Gray's "Elegy Written in a Country Churchyard."

Enjambment: The continuation of a complete idea (a sentence or clause) from one line or couplet of a poem to the next line or couplet without a pause. An example of enjambment can be found in the first line of Joyce Kilmer's poem *Trees:* "I think that I shall never see/ A poem as lovely as a tree." *Enjambment* comes from the French word for "to straddle

Envoy: The shorter final stanza of a poem, as in a ballade.

Epic: A long, serious poem that tells the story of a heroic figure. Two of the most famous epic poems are the *Iliad* and the *Odyssey* by Homer, which tell about the Trojan War and the adventures of Odysseus on his voyage home after the war.

Epigram: A very short, witty poem: "Sir, I admit your general rule,/That every poet is a fool,/But you yourself may serve to show it,/That every fool is not a poet." (Samuel Taylor Coleridge)

Epithalamium (or epithalamion): A poem in honor of a bride and bridegroom.

Feminine rhyme: A rhyme that occurs in a final unstressed syllable: *pleasure/leisure, longing/yearning*.

figure of speech: A verbal expression in which words or

sounds are arranged in a particular way to achieve a particular effect. Figures of speech are organized into different categories, such as alliteration, assonance, metaphor, metonymy, onomatopoeia, simile, and synecdoche.

Free verse (also vers libre): Poetry composed of either rhymed or unrhymed lines that have no set meter.

Hyperbole: A figure of speech in which deliberate exaggeration is used for emphasis. Many everyday expressions are examples of hyperbole: *tons of money, waiting for ages, a flood of tears,* etc. Hyperbole is the opposite of litotes.

Iambic pentameter: A type of meter in poetry, in which there are five iambs to a line. (The prefix *penta-* means "five," as in *pentagon*, a geometrical figure with five sides. *Meter* refers to rhythmic units. In a line of iambic pentameter, there are five rhythmic units that are iambs.) Shakespeare's plays were written mostly in iambic pentameter, which is the most common type of meter in English poetry. An example of an iambic pentameter line from Shakespeare's *Romeo and Juliet* is "But **soft**!/ What **light**/ through **yon**/ der **win**/dow **breaks**?" Another, from *Richard III,* is "A **horse**!/ A **horse**!/ My **king**/dom **for**/ a **horse**!" (The stressed syllables are in bold.)

Idyll, or idyl: Either a short poem depicting a peaceful, idealized country scene, or a long poem that tells a story about heroic deeds or extraordinary events set in the distant past. *Idylls of the King,* by Alfred Lord Tennyson, is about King Arthur and the Knights of the Round Table.

Lay: A long narrative poem, especially one that was sung by medieval minstrels called trouvères. The *Lais* of Marie de France are lays.

Limerick: A light, humorous poem of five usually anapestic lines with the rhyme scheme of *aabba*.

Litotes: A figure of speech in which a positive is stated by negating its opposite. Some examples of litotes: *no small victory, not a bad idea, not unhappy*. Litotes is the opposite of hyperbole.

Lyric: A poem, such as a sonnet or an ode, that expresses the thoughts and feelings of the poet. A lyric poem may resemble a song in form or style.

Masculine rhyme: A rhyme that occurs in a final stressed syllable: *cat/hat, desire/fire, observe/deserve.*

Metaphor: A figure of speech in which two things are compared, usually by saying one thing is another, or by substituting a more descriptive word for the more common or usual word that would be expected. Some examples of metaphors: *the world's a stage, he was a lion in battle, drowning in debt,* and *a sea of troubles.*

Meter: The arrangement of a line of poetry by the number of syllables and the rhythm of accented (or stressed) syllables.

Metonymy: A figure of speech in which one word is substituted for another with which it is closely associated. For example, in the expression *The pen is mightier than the sword,* the word *pen* is used for "the written word," and *sword* is used for "military power."

Narrative: Telling a story. Ballads, epics, and lays are different kinds of narrative poems.

Ode: A lyric poem that is serious and thoughtful in tone and has a very precise, formal structure. John Keats's "Ode on a Grecian Urn" is a famous example of this type of poem.

Onomatopoeia: A figure of speech in which words are used to imitate sounds. Examples of onomatopoeic words are *buzz, hiss, zing, clippety-clop,* and *tick-tock.* Keats's "Ode to a Nightingale" not only uses onomatopoeia, but calls our attention to it: "Forlorn! The very word is like a bell/To toll me back from thee to my sole self!" Another example of onomatopoeia is found in this line from Tennyson's *Come Down, O Maid:* "The moan of doves in immemorial elms,/And murmuring of innumerable bees." The repeated "m/n" sounds reinforce the idea of "murmuring" by imitating the hum of insects on a warm summer day.

Ottava rima: A type of poetry consisting of 10- or 11-syllable lines arranged in 8-line "octaves" with the rhyme scheme *abababcc*.

Pastoral: A poem that depicts rural life in a peaceful, idealized way.

Pentameter: A line of poetry that has five metrical feet.

Personification: A figure of speech in which things or abstract ideas are given human attributes: *dead leaves dance in the wind, blind justice.*

Poetry: A type of literature that is written in meter.

Quatrain: A stanza or poem of four lines.

Refrain: A line or group of lines that is repeated throughout a poem, usually after every stanza.

Rhyme: The occurrence of the same or similar sounds at the end of two or more words. When the rhyme occurs in a final stressed syllable, it is said to be masculine: *cat / hat, desire / fire, observe / deserve.* When the rhyme occurs in a final unstressed syllable, it is said to be feminine: *longing / yearning.* The pattern of rhyme in a stanza or poem is shown usually by using a different letter for each final sound. In a poem with an *aabba* rhyme scheme, the first, second, and fifth lines end in one sound, and the third and fourth lines end in another.

Rhyme royal: A type of poetry consisting of stanzas of seven lines in iambic pentameter with the rhyme scheme *ababbcc*. Rhyme royal was an innovation introduced by Geoffrey Chaucer.

Romanticism: The principles and ideals of the Romantic

movement in literature and the arts during the late 18th and early 19th centuries. Romanticism, which was a reaction to the classicism of the early 18th century, favored feeling over reason and placed great emphasis on the subjective, or personal, experience of the individual. Nature was also a major theme. The great English Romantic poets include Wordsworth, Coleridge, Byron, Shelley, and Keats.

Scansion: The analysis of a poem's meter. This is usually done by marking the stressed and unstressed syllables in each line and then, based on the pattern of the stresses, dividing the line into feet.

Senryu: A short Japanese poem that is similar to a haiku in structure but treats human beings rather than nature, often in a humorous or satiric way.

Simile:A figure of speech in which two things are compared using the word "like" or "as." An example of a simile using *like* occurs in Langston Hughes's poem "Harlem": "What happens to a dream deferred?/ Does it dry up/ like a raisin in the sun?"

Sonnet: A lyric poem that is 14 lines long. Italian (or Petrarchan) sonnets are divided into two quatrains and a six-line "sestet," with the rhyme scheme *abba abba cdecde* (or *cdcdcd*). English (or Shakespearean) sonnets are composed of three quatrains and a final couplet, with a rhyme scheme of *abab cdcd efef gg*. English sonnets are written generally in iambic pentameter.

Spondee: A metrical foot of two syllables, both of which are long (or stressed).

Stanza: Two or more lines of poetry that together form one of the divisions of a poem. The stanzas of a poem are usually of the same length and follow the same pattern of meter and rhyme.

Synecdoche: A figure of speech in which a part is used to designate the whole or the whole is used to designate a part. For example, the phrase "all hands on deck" means "all men on deck," not just their hands. The reverse situation, in which the whole is used for a part, occurs in the sentence "The U.S. beat Russia in the final game," where the U.S. and Russia stand for "the U.S. team" and "the Russian team," respectively.

Terza rima: A type of poetry consisting of 10- or 11-syllable lines arranged in three-line "tercets" with the rhyme scheme *aba bcb cdc,* etc. The poet Dante is credited with inventing terza rima, which he used in his *Divine Comedy.* Terza rima was borrowed into English by Chaucer, and it has been used by many English poets, including Milton, Shelley, and Auden.

Trochee:A metrical foot of two syllables, one long (or stressed) and one short (or unstressed). An easy way to remember the trochee is to memorize the first line of a lighthearted poem by Samuel Taylor Coleridge, which demonstrates the use of various kinds of metrical feet: "**Trochee**/ **trips** from/ **long** to/ **short**." (The stressed syllables are in bold.) The trochee is the reverse of the iamb.

Bibliography

Abrams, M.H., *Natural Supernaturalism: Tradition and Revolution in Romantic Literature*, New York: W.W. Norton, 1973.

Abrams, Meyer H. *Natural Supernaturalism: Tradition and Revolution in Romantic Literature.* New York: Norton, 1971.

Abrams, Meyer H. *The Mirror and the Lamp*. London: O. U. P., 1971.

Baillie, Joanna. Letter, 5 Feb 1824, Wellcome Library for the History and Understanding of Medicine, London.

Bate, Jonathan. John Clare: A biography; Farrar, Straus and Giroux, 2003.

Behler, Ernst. *Unendliche Perfektabilität: Europäische Romantik und Französische Revolution.* Paderborn, Germany: Schöningh, 1989.

Beiser, Frederick C. *Enlightenment, Revolution and Romanticism: The Genesis of Modern German Political Thought, 1790–1800.* Cambridge, Mass.: Harvard University Press, 1992.

Bentley, Gerald Eades and Bentley Jr., G. *William Blake: The Critical Heritage*. 1995, pp. 34-5.

Berlin, Isaiah. *The Roots of Romanticism*. London: Chatto & Windus, 1999.

Bindman, David. "Blake as a Painter" in *The Cambridge Companion to William Blake*, Morris Eaves (ed.), Cambridge, 2003, p. 106

Bjork, Robert E. and John D. Niles, editors. *A Beowulf Handbook*. Exeter: U of Exeter P, 1997.

Bjork, Robert E., editor. *Cynewulf: Basic Readings*. Volume 4 of Basic Readings in Anglo-Saxon England. New York: Garland P, 1996.

Blake, William, 1984. *Blake's "America, a Prophecy" ; And, "Europe, a Prophecy"*.

Bliss, A. J. *The Metre of Beowulf*. 2nd edition. Oxford: Blackwell, 1967.

Bosworth, Joseph, T. Northcote Toller, and Alistair Campbell. *An Anglo-Saxon Dictionary*. Vol 2: Supplement by T.N. Toller; Vol. 3: Enlarged Addenda and Corrigenda by A. Campell to the Supplement by T.N. Toller. Oxford: Oxford UP, 1882-98, 1908-21, 1972.

Bradley, S.A.J. *Anglo-Saxon Poetry*. Everyman's Library. London: Dent, 1982.

Breckman, Warren, *European Romanticism: A Brief History with Documents*. New York: Bedford/St. Martin's, 2007.

Brunner, Karl. *Altenglische Grammatik nach der angelsächsischen Grammatik von Eduard Sievers*. 3rd edition. Tübingen: Max Niemeyer Verlag, 1964.

Burns, Robert. Bold, Alan. ed. *Rhymer Rab: An Anthology of Poems and Prose*. London: Black Swan, 1993.

Butler, Marilyn. *Romantics, Rebels and Reactionaries: English Literature and its Background, 1760–1830*. Oxford: Oxford University Press, 1982.

Cable, Thomas. *The English Alliterative Tradition*. Middle Ages Series. Philadelphia: U of Pennsylvania P, 1991.

Calder, Daniel G. and Michael J. Allen, editors. *Sources and Analogues of Old English Poetry: The Major Latin Texts in Translation*. Cambridge: D. S. Brewer, 1976.

Calder, Daniel G. et al., editors. *Sources and Analogues of Old English Poetry II: The Major Germanic and Celtic Texts in Translation*. Cambridge: D. S. Brewer, 1983.

Campbell, James, Eric John, and Patrick Wormald. *The Anglo-Saxons*. Oxford: Phaidon, 1982.

Carhart, Margaret S. *The Life and Work of Joanna Baillie*. New Haven: Yale University Press, 1923.

Carswell, Donald. *Sir Walter: A Four-Part Study in Biography (Scott, Hogg, Lockhart, Joanna Baillie)*. John Murray: London, 1930.

Chambers, R. W., Max Förster, and Robin Flower, editors. *The Exeter Book of Old English Poetry*. London: P. Lund, 1933.

Ciofalo, John J. "The Ascent of Genius in the Court and Academy." *The Self-Portraits of Francisco Goya*. Cambridge University Press, 2001.

Clark Hall, John R. *A Concise Anglo-Saxon Dictionary*. With a supplement by Herbert D. Meritt. 4th edition. Cambridge: Cambridge UP, 1960.

Clarke, Norma. 'Baillie, Joanna (1762–1851)', *Oxford Dictionary of National Biography*. Oxford: Oxford University Press, Sept 2004; online edn, Jan 2006 accessed 5 Oct 2006

Cousin, John William. *A Short Biographical Dictionary of English Literature*. London, J. M. Dent & Sons; New York, E. P. Dutton, 1910.

Curran, Stuart, ed. *The Cambridge Companion to British Romanticism*. Cambridge, U.K.: Cambridge University Press, 1993.

De Man, Paul. *The Rhetoric of Romanticism*. New York: Columbia University Press, 1984.

Dietrich Hohmann: *Ich, Robert Burns*, Biographical Novel, Neues Leben, Berlin 1990 (in German)

Donner, H.W., ed. *Plays and Poems of Thomas Lovell Beddoes* (London: Routledge and Kegan Paul Ltd., 1950).

Donoghue, Daniel. *Style in Old English Poetry: The Test*

of the Auxiliary. Volume 196 of Yale Studies in English. New Haven: Yale UP, 1987.

Eaves, Morris. *The Counter Arts Conspiracy: Art and Industry in the Age of Blake*. Ithaca and London: Cornell University Press, 1992.

Elizabeth A. Bray, *Discovery of the Hebrides*. Birlinn Publishers, 1999.

Ewton, Ralph W., Jr. *The Literary Theories of August Wilhelm Schlegel*. The Hague: Mouton, 1972.

Favret, Mary A., and Watson, Nicola J., eds. *At the Limits of Romanticism: Essays in Cultural, Feminist, and Materialist Criticism*. Bloomington: Indiana University Press, 1994.

Fay,Elizabeth, *Romantic Medievalism. History and the Romantic Literary Ideal*. Houndsmills, Basingstoke: Palgrave, 2002.

Feldman, Paula R., and Kelley, Theresa M., eds. *Romantic Women Writers: Voices and Controversies*. Hanover, N.H.: University Press of New England, 1995.

Fell, Christine E. *Women in Anglo-Saxon England*. London: British Museum Publications, 1984.

Firchow, Peter. *Introduction. Friedrich Schlegel, Lucinde and the Fragments* [section 2A, above: 1971]. 3-39.

Flower, Robin and Hugh Smith, editors. *The Parker Chronicle and Laws*. Volume 208 of Early English Text Society. London: Oxford UP, 1941.

Forstman, Jack. *A Romantic Triangle: Schleiermacher and Early German Romanticism. Missoula*, MT: Scholars, 1977.

Fowler, Alastair. *The History of English Literature*. Cambridge, MA: Harvard University Press, 1989.

Frank, Frederick S. *The First Gothics: A Critical Guide to the English Gothic Novel*. New York: Garland, 1987.

Friedlaender, Walter, *David to Delacroix*, (Originally published in German; reprinted 1980) 1952.

Fulk, R. D. *A History of Old English Meter*. Middle Ages Series. Philadelphia: U of Pennsylvania P, 1992.

Fulk, R. D., editor. *Interpretations of Beowulf: A Critical Anthology*. Bloomington and Indianapolis: Indiana UP, 1991.

Garmonsway, G. N. and Jacqueline Simpson, editors. *Beowulf and Its Analogues*. London: Dent, 1969.

Geoffrey Summerfield, Hugh Haughton, Adam Phillips, "John Clare in context", Cambridge University Press, 1994,

Geoffrey Summerfield, in introduction to *John Clare: Selected Poems*, Penguin Books 1990, pp 13–22.

Godden, Malcolm and Michael Lapidge, editors. *The Cambridge Companion to Old English Literature*. Cambridge: Cambridge UP, 1991.

Gollancz, Israel, editor. *The Cædmon Manuscript of Anglo-Saxon Biblical Poetry*. Oxford: Oxford UP, 1927.

Gordon, R. K. *Anglo-Saxon Poetry*. Everyman's Library. London: Dent, 1954.

Greenfield, Stanley B. and Daniel G. Calder. *A New Critical History of Old English Literature*. Includes a survey of the Anglo-Latin background by Michael Lapidge. New York and London: New York University P, 1986.

Greenfield, Stanley B. and Fred C. Robinson. *A Bibliography of Publications on Old English Literature to the End of 1972*. Toronto: U of Toronto P, 1980.

Grewe, Cordula, *Painting the Sacred in the Age of German Romanticism*. Burlington: Ashgate, 2009.

Gutwirth, Madelyn, Avriel Goldberger, and Karyna Szmurlo, eds. *Germaine de Staël: Crossing the Borders*. New Brunswick, N.J.: Rutgers University Press, 1991.

Hale, Margaret R. "Introduction: The Horn of Oberon" [section 2A, above, under Jean Paul, School for Aesthetics: 1973]. xvii-lx, 316-24.

Handwerk, Gary. *Irony and Ethics in Narrative: From Schlegel to Lacan*. New Haven: Yale UP, 1985.

Hannah, Richard W. *The Fichtean Dynamic of Novalis' Poetics*. Bern: Lang, 1981.

Hare, Augustus J.C. *The Life and Letters of Maria Edgeworth*. 2 vols. London: Edward Arnold, 1894.

Hasenfratz, Robert J. *Beowulf Scholarship: An Annotated Bibliography, 1979-1990*. Volume 14 of Garland medieval bibliographies. New York: Garland P, 1993.

Haswell-Smith, Hamish. *The Scottish Islands*. Edinburgh: Canongate, 2004.

Healey, Antonette diPaolo and Richard L. Venezky. *A Microfiche Concordance to Old English*. Toronto: Dictionary of Old English Project, 1980.

Hogg, Richard M. *A Grammar of Old English*. Oxford and Cambridge, Mass.: Blackwell, 1992.

Holmes, Richard. *The Age of Wonder: The Romantic Generation and the Discovery of the Beauty and Terror of Science*. 2009.

Holthausen, F. *Altenglisches etymologisches Wörterbuch*. 2nd edition. Heidelberg: Carl Winter, 1963.

Honour, Hugh, *Romanticism*, (Westview Press) 1979.

Horwitz, Barbara J. *British Women Writers, 1700-1850: An Annotated Bibliography of Their Works and Works about Them*. Lanham, MD: The Scarecrow Press and Pasadena, CA: Salem Press, 1997.

Hunter Blair, Peter. *An Introduction to Anglo-Saxon England*. 2nd edition. Cambridge: Cambridge UP, 1977.

Izenberg, Gerald N. *Impossible Individuality: Romanticism, Revolution and the Origins of Modern Selfhood, 1787–1802*. Princeton, N.J.: Princeton University Press, 1992.

Karkov, Catherine E., editor. *The Archaeology of Anglo-Saxon England: Basic Readings*. Volume 7 of Basic Readings in Anglo-Saxon England. New York: Garland P, 1999.

Ker, N. R. *Catalogue of Manuscripts Containing Anglo-Saxon*. See also Ker 1976. Oxford: Clarendon P, 1957.

Kiernan, Kevin S., editor. *The Electronic Beowulf*. Ann Arbor: U. of Michigan P, 2000.

Klaeber, F., editor. *Beowulf and the Fight at Finnsburg*. Includes two supplements. 3rd edition. Boston: D.C. Heath, 1950.

Krapp, George Philip and Elliott Van Kirk Dobbie, editors. *The Anglo-Saxon Poetic Records*. New York: Columbia UP, 1931-1953.

Lapidge, Michael, John Blair, Simon Keynes, and Donald Scragg, editors. *The Blackwell Encyclopaedia of Anglo-Saxon England*. Oxford: Basil Blackwell, 1999.

Lass, Roger. *Old English: A Historical Linguistic Companion*. Cambridge: Cambridge UP, 1994.

Letter to the Guardian: Robinson's most recent public declaration of ownership of copyright, February 2003.

Lim, Cwisfa, *Romanticism - The dawn of a new era*, 2002. (reprinted 2006)

Lucas, E.V. *Highways and byways in Sussex*. Macmillan, 1904.

Magoun, Francis P. "The Oral-Formulaic Character of {Anglo-Saxon} Narrative Poetry." *Speculum* 28 (1953): 446-67.

Marcel, Brion. *Art of the Romantic Era*. Henry Holt & Company, Inc., 1966.

Margaret Grainger (ed), "The natural history prose writings of John Clare", *Oxford English Texts*, Oxford University Press, 1983.

Marsha Keith Schuchard, *Why Mrs Blake Cried: Swedenborg, Blake and the Sexual Basis of Spiritual Vision*, pp. 1-20

Marshall, Peter. *William Blake: Visionary Anarchist* (Revised Edition ed.). Freedom Press, 1994.

Mary Ann Dobratz. "The Works of "Fiona MacLeod" Notes to First Edition", 2000.

Masson, Scott, 'Romanticism', Ch.7 in *The Oxford Handbook of English Literature and Theology*, (Oxford University Press) 2007.

Mazzeno, Laurence W. *The British Novel 1680-1832: An Annotated Bibliography*. Lanham, MD: The Scarecrow Press and Pasadena, CA: Salem Press, 1997.

McGann, J. "Did Blake Betray the French Revolution", *Presenting Poetry: Composition, Publication, Reception*, Cambridge University Press, 1995, p.128

Mellor, Anne K., *Romanticism and Gender*. New York: Routledge, 1993.

Mellor, Anne K., ed. *Romanticism and Feminism*. Bloomington: Indiana University Press, 1988.

Mitchell, Bruce and Fred C. Robinson. *A Guide to Old English*. 5th edition. Oxford: Blackwell, 1992.

Murray, Christopher, ed. *Encyclopedia of the Romantic Era, 1760-1850* (2 vol 2004); 850 articles by experts; 1600pp

O'Keeffe, Katherine O'Brien, editor. *Reading Old English Texts*. Cambridge: Cambridge UP, 1997.

Pipkin, James, ed. *English and German Romanticism: Cross-Currents and Controversies*. Heidelberg, Germany: C. Winter, 1985.

Pope, John C. and R. D., Fulk, editors. *Eight Old English Poems*. 3rd edition. New York: W. W. Norton, 2000.

Raine, Kathleen *World of Art: William Blake*. Thames & Hudson, 1970.

Rajan, Tilottama. *Dark Interpreter: The Discourse of Romanticism*. Ithaca, N.Y.: Cornell University Press, 1980.

Reidhead et. al., "Norton Anthology of English Literature,"The Romantic Period - Volume D" (W.W. Norton & Company Ltd.) 2006

Robinson, Orrin W. *Old English and Its Closest Relatives: A Survey of the Earliest Germanic Languages*. Stanford: Stanford UP, 1992.

Sales, Roger, *John Clare: A Literary Life*; Palgrave Macmillian, 2002.

Schenk, H.G., *The Mind of the European Romantics: An Essay in Cultural History*, (Constable) 1966.

Sheila Rowbotham's *Edward Carpenter: A Life of Liberty and Love* p. 135

Short, Douglas D. *Beowulf Scholarship: An Annotated Bibliography*. Volume 193 of Garland reference library of the humanities. New York: Garland P, 1980.

Simpson, David. Wordsworth's Historical Imagination: The Poetry of Displacement. New York: Methuen, 1987.

Swanton, Michael. *Anglo-Saxon Prose*. 2nd edition. London: Dent, 1993.

Tom Hayes, "William Blake's AndrogYnous EGO-Ideal," *ELH*, 71(1), 141-165 (2004).

Tucker, "Jane Austen's Family", 147; Le Faye, *Family Record*, 43–44.

Whitelock, Dorothy, editor. *Sweet's Anglo-Saxon Reader in Prose and Verse*. 15th edition. Oxford: Oxford UP, 1975.

Workman, Leslie J., "Medievalism and Romanticism," *Poetica* 39–40 (1994): 1–34.

Index